TENKO!

RANGOON JAIL

THE AMAZING STORY OF SGT. JOHN BOYD'S SURVIVAL AS A POW IN A NOTORIOUS JAPANESE PRISON CAMP

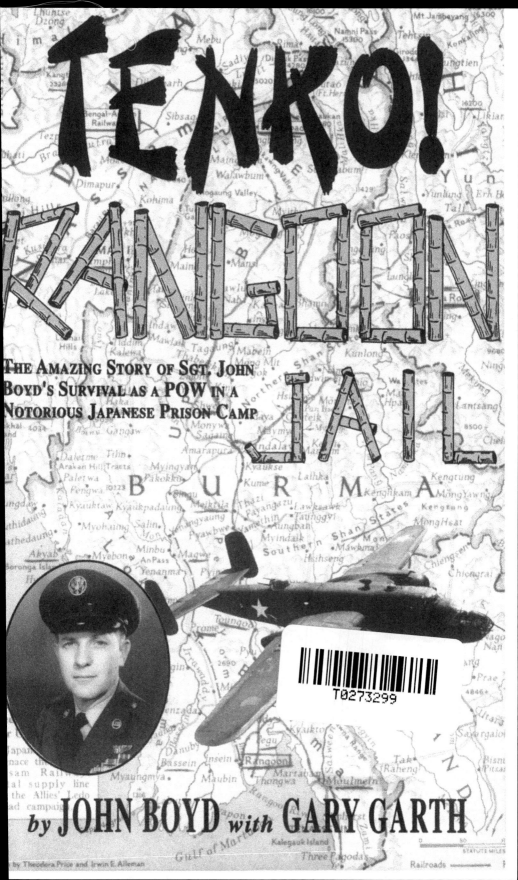

by JOHN BOYD with GARY GARTH

TURNER PUBLISHING COMPANY
412 Broadway
P.O. Box 3101
Paducah, KY 42002-3101
(502) 443-0121

Turner Publishing Company Staff:
Publishing Consultant: Douglas W. Sikes
Projector Coordinator: David Figge
Designer: Herbert C. Banks II

Author: John Boyd

Library of Congress Cataolg Card Number: 96-60245
ISBN 978-1-63026-972-2

Limited Edition.

Table of Contents

Dedication: "Our Fallen Comrades"

Freedom is not easy. Ever since Cain killed Able the world has always held vicious and aggressive people who try to oppress and enslave other people.

Everything in this world of value has a price. Jesus Christ paid the price for our spiritual freedom with his death, burial and resurrection. But while we sojourn on this earth our fallen comrades have paid the price for the freedom that we enjoy while walking the course of this life.

The lust of the flesh, the lust of the eye and the pride of life will control the character of some people, and I suppose that this shall always be true until Christ puts all enemies under his feet and returns the kingdom to God.

Before any victory can be obtained, before any war can be won, so many lives must be given for freedom. The survivors of the Rangoon Prison Camp may have suffered, but we did not pay the supreme price. We are, however, the recipients of this freedom that our fallen comrades so gallantly have given us.

This book is dedicated to these young men and women, many of whom never reached the age of 21, who died for our freedom. I think of them daily. Their faces remain fresh in my memory.

It is my prayer that the leaders of this great nation will forever maintain the strength necessary to preserve and secure the freedom that our fallen comrades have given us, and that we will forever cherish this heritage.

John W. Boyd

Acknowledgements

My thanks to John Boyd, who allowed me a glimpse inside the Rangoon Central Jail to meet some of the men who answered when their country called. They were men from another generation- my father's generation- but their unselfish sacrifices helped pave the way for the freedoms we enjoy today.

Their efforts must never be forgotten.

My unending thanks, gratitude and love to my wife, Katy, a woman of faith who lead me to Christ. You are my companion and friend. Thank you for your patience, encouragement, guidance and enduring love.

Gary Garth
Murray, Kentucky
February 1996

Preface

I spent 21 months in the Japanese prisoner of war camp in Rangoon, Burma before being liberated by the British 14th Army on May 3, 1945. However, this is not just the story of one man's experience. It is the story of how men of different nationalities - Americans, British, Indians, Chinese and Karens - came together in the prison camp to help one another. It is also a true story of survival, faith, friendship, toughness, loyalty, faithfulness and luck. The bond forged between men and nations was, and remains, firm. While imprisoned in Rangoon the desire for freedom and concern for the group's safety was foremost in every man's heart. Life in the Rangoon Central Jail was a fight for survival, but it was not every man for himself. The sacrifices that men made for one another, some hardly known to each other, are told in this story.

All the men suffered and many died as prisoners of war in the Rangoon City Jail, which the Japanese used as a notorious prisoner of war compound from 1942 to 1945.

Several books have been written about the Rangoon prisoner of war camp. These include *The Flame of Freedom* by Robert Hammond, *Operation: Rangoon Jail* by Colonel K. P. MacKenzie, *All Hell on the Irrawaddy* by John Tim Finerty, *The Rats of Rangoon* by Lionel Hudson, and *Grandfather Long Legs* by Ian Morrison.

The Rangoon Central Jail was located in the southwest section of the city of Rangoon. The prison was bound on the north by St. Johns Road, on the south by Commissioners Road, on the east by Pongyi Street and on the west by Keigh Lry Street. The jail was also located two and one half blocks from the Rangoon harbor and docks, which during the last two years of the war were subjected to almost constant bombardment from American and British air power. The prison camp was hit three times during these bombing raids. These stray bombs killed some American, English and Indian prisoners along with several Japanese guards.

There were approximately 1,200 allied prisoners of war in the Rangoon Central Jail. These included about 150 Americans and 350 British. The rest were Indian and Chinese. There was no hospital in the prison camp other than a sparse room designated as such. Sick and injured men received virtually no medical care. The precise prisoner death rate is unknown but it has been estimated that between 1942 and 1945 roughly 40 to 50 percent of the prisoner population died as a result of malnutrition, beri-beri, dysentery, malaria, jungle sores, small pox, diphtheria, a cholera epidemic, torture, allied aircraft bombings, lack of medical treatment and assassination. Death was a grim and daily companion.

Dysentery was probably the most wide spread illness. One case was reported by actual count of a British POW who had 254 bowel movements during a period of three days. He died on the morning of the fourth day. A prisoner was not classified as having dysentery unless his waste contained both blood and mucus. Otherwise it was considered diarrhea. The men also suffered from septic sores. These septic sores, best described as scab-covered puss pockets, were called "scabies" until they dug deep into the flesh. They were then classified as jungle sores.

Prisoner morale generally remained high even under the very worst conditions. I spent 84 days in solitary confinement before being moved to cell block number six where the death rate among about 100 prisoners was sometimes two or three men per day. We were also forced into hard labor building air raid shelters, digging slit trenches, unloading rice barges and railroad cars, and other work.

I was a technical sergeant, radio operator and gunner on a B-25 with the 22nd Bomb Squadron, 10th Air Force, Chakulia, India. I was shot down over Meikteila, Burma on August 3, 1943 while flying my 43rd mission.

I survived a death sentence, was almost bayoneted, suffered from dysentery, beri-beri, jungle sores and scabies and served as "huncho" (the Japanese term for noncommissioned officer in charge) in the prison camp and on work parties. Other men in the camp suffered far more than I.

In this story you'll meet Roy Anthony Stephen "Ras" Pagani, who survived a brutal tale of escape and adventure before his arrival in the Rangoon Central Jail. This is also the story, in part, of Colonel K. P. MacKenzie, a British doctor from the Royal Army Medical Corps, 17th Division, 45th Brigade. Colonel MacKenzie had served in France during World War I. He was captured by the Japanese on February 21, 1942, and spent more than three years in the Rangoon prison.

The story will include the work and efforts of Captain Brahmanath N. Sudan, who was in the British service of the Burma Army Medical Corps. The services of Captain Sudan were received by men of all nations in the prison camp. Had it not been for his care I very likely would have died. Other men whose Rangoon experiences are entered here include Sergeant John E. Leisure, who was shot down with me on August 3, 1943. Leisure and I spent 84 days together in solitary confinement. Other men in the camp included Chinese Major General H. C. Chi, Captain Walter E. Cotton, a B-24 pilot and one of the few Americans in Rangoon when I arrived, James Masterson, Bud Costic, Donald Humphreys, Jack Horner, Perry Marshall, Don Davis, Charles Perry, Bill Thomas, Douglas Gilbert, Gene Lutz, Nigel Loring, Leo Frank, Leland Ramsey and Harold Goad.

I would also like to thank Hugh Crumpler for his background information about Major General Caleb Haynes. I agree with Mr. Crumpler that General Haynes never received the recognition that he deserved, and that he was truly one of the greatest flying generals of all time.

These are just a few of the of the people who will be mentioned here. Hundreds more were held at Rangoon. Good men, all, with each one rendering enormous help to his fellow prisoners.

Our struggle for freedom inside the Rangoon Prison ended on May 3, 1945 when we were liberated by the British 14th Army. But the Burmese struggle for freedom continues today. The Karen Nation that fought with Major Hugh Seagrim and who helped Ras Pagani with his escape attempt through southern Burma continues today to lead the fight for freedom and a democratic way of life.

The Burmese quest for freedom received a bright spark in 1947 when Burmese General Aung San, who is sometimes referred to as "Burma's George Washington" negotiated Burma's independence from the British. However, Aung San was assassinated that same year and the country then came under the control of 21 military officers which formed Burma's military junta. Through terror and a bizarre form of socialism the junta has controlled the country for almost a half century.

General Aung San's daughter, Aung San Suu Kyi, was two when her father was assassinated. She left Burma at age 15 but returned to her homeland in March 1988 to care for her dying mother. That same year Suu Kyi entered into a pro-democracy revolution against Burma's military dictator and in the months that followed her enormous popularity threatened to topple the military government.

On August 8, 1988 soldiers were ordered to quiet the pro-democracy movement and demonstrations. The bloody crackdown killed more than 3,000 students, religious leaders and other civilians. Then on August 26, before the gold-domed Shwedago pagoda in Rangoon, Suu Kyi first spoke publicly against government oppression and vowed to carry on her father's mission of freeing Burma from political oppression and strife.

Swayed by pressure of the growing democracy movement the mili-

In 1995, a motion picture titled Beyond Rangoon accurately presented the situation in Burma today. It provided a true account of Burma's struggle for freedom. However, the movie depicted an American female doctor who was working to help the Karen people. This aspect of the movie was untrue. This photo is of Dr. Cynthia Maung, for whom the character could have been based upon. "Dr. Cynthia" has devoted her life to the cause of the Karen people by bringing health care to endangered populations in the war-torn mountains.

tary government promised to hold a democratic election for a new national parliament. Suu Kyi and two other politicians formed the National League for Democracy (NLD). Suu Kyi traveled tirelessly around the country in support of NLD candidates before the military government, sighting violations of "security laws," placed her under house arrest on July 20, 1989.

Suu Kyi's incarceration did not slow the democratic ground swell. The seeds for democracy had been well sown and during the May 1990 election the NLD won 81 percent of the parliamentary seats. The military junta, however, refused to relinquish their power. Suu Kyi spent six years at 54 University Avenue in Rangoon under house arrest not far from the Rangoon Central Jail where we were held prisoners of war by the Japanese. While under detention she won the 1944 Nobel Peace Prize.

Burma is now known as Myanmar and the city of Rangoon has been renamed Yangon. But the struggle for Burmese freedom continues as it did when Major Seagrim and the Karens successfully fought the Japanese. Along with Suu Kyi and many other freedom supporters, Dr. Cynthia Maung works to bring health care to the people of the war-torn mountains where they are viewed as heroes and heroines. It is a relationship similar to the one Major Hugh Seagrim shared with the Karen people.

The Karens assisted a student uprising in 1988 and many students joined the Karen movement after the government's assault to squash the pro-democracy movement. In the last half century the brave people of this Christian nation, who fought with the United States and England throughout World War II, have been all but neglected by the United States and the United Nations in their long struggle for freedom.

Burma's freedom was not obtained when Suu Kyi's father, Aung San, negotiated Burma's independence from the British in 1947 and he was assassinated the same year. The country was then taken over by 21 generals who constitute Burma's military junta which has controlled the country to this day.

General Aung San's daughter, Aung San Suu Kyi and Michael Aris of British nationality were married on January 1, 1972 and they settled in Oxford. Suu Kyi, the mother of two sons returned to Rangoon in March 1988 to care for her dying mother and the same year entered into a pro-democracy revolution against Burma's military dictator, General Ne Win who ruled the country for 26 years through terror and a bizarre form of socialism. Over the next year, her popularity threatened to topple the military government.

On August 8, 1988, soldiers were ordered to put down the demonstration; over the next few days, they killed 3,000 students, monks, and others. On August 26, Suu Kyi yielded to pressure and decided to speak out against the government. Hundreds of thousands of people settled before the gold domed Shwedago Pagoda in Rangoon. When Suu Kyi began to speak, the half million people were astonished that she looked and spoke exactly like her famous father. After ten minutes, she vowed to take up her father's mission of freeing Burma from oppression. The government responded by placing her under house arrest at 54 University Avenue in Rangoon on July 20, 1989. While under detention, she won the Nobel Peace Prize in 1994.

Swayed by the pressure of the growing democracy movement, the military promised to hold a democratic election for a new national parliament. Then, Suu Kyi and two other politicians formed the National League for Democracy (NLD). Suu Kyi went across the country, making up to 25 speeches a day. She dazzled the crowds and soon became a prominent figure. During the election of 1990, the NLD won 81 percent of the seats in parliament. However, the military junta would not relinquish their power. Since Suu Kyi;s release, she has continued to work for the freedom of Burma.

The Karen Nation has continued to lead the fight for freedom since the military government took power in 1947. The Karens helped the college students in the uprising in 1988. Many of the students joined the Karen movement after they were driven from Burma. This Christian nation who fought with the United States and England through World War II, has been neglected by the United States and the United Nations in their struggle for freedom. (Please see the Appendix for a detailed description of the major ethnic groups that comprise Burma today.)

Our Lord Jesus Christ said, "Greater love has no man than this, that he lay down his life for a friend." Some of the men in the Rangoon Prison Camp gave their lives for their friends and comrades. I was fortunate to survive and as I count my blessings each day I remain indebted to each of my fellow POWs. Without their courage, sacrifice, strength and support I would not be here.

Introduction

Meiktila, Burma. August 3, 1943.

It was called skip bombing, a maneuver that required the twin-engine B-25 to make a straight line, low-level target approach near tree top level. This allowed the pilot to "slide" the bombs into the target. It also made the airplane an easy mark for anti-aircraft fire.

This day two planes from the 22nd bomb squadron based in Chakulia, India and a third plane from 490th squadron based in Kurmitola, India were directed to a site near Japanese-held Meiktila, Burma. The mission: to destroy a dam on the Irrawaddy River system.

Technical Sergeant John W. Boyd, a 24-year-old radio operator from Mayfield, Kentucky, was aboard the trailing plane. Boyd was well-seasoned in Burma-China-India Theater action. He was flying his 43rd mission and expected to be transferred back to the United States within next two months.

On this run Boyd was not with his regular flight crew, having substituted for a fellow radio man who had previously taken Boyd's slot while the Kentuckian was on leave. Lieutenant Charles McCook was piloting the plane. Along with McCook and Boyd the six-man crew included co-pilot Nathaniel L. Hightower, navigator Henry J. Carlin, engineer-gunner John E. Leisure and turret gunner Sidney Burke.

Although the bombing run was well guarded by ground fire the first two bombers delivered their loads without incident. Lieutenant McCook brought his B-25 down to 1,500 feet then dropped near the forest canopy and began the run toward the dam. Sitting with his back to the bomb bay compartment and facing the tail of the aircraft, Boyd could look though the belly gun opening and the side window and see the "tat-tat-tat-tat-tat" flash from the anti-aircraft fire.

The plane was suddenly rocked by an explosion. McCook immediately pulled the crippled aircraft to about 1,000 feet but in the few seconds it took to reach that altitude the heat from the fire sent a searing draft through the tail of the plane. Ground fire had hit the bomb bay compartment. The fire quickly burned through the intercom wiring that linked the pilot, co-pilot and navigator to the crew in the tail of the aircraft. McCook and Hightower struggled to keep the crippled B-25 airborne while searching for a suitable spot to attempt a crash landing. Boyd, Leisure and Burke prepared to jump.

Leisure jumped first, executing the emergency jumping procedure to textbook perfection. Boyd slipped on his own parachute then helped Burke into his.

McCook now had the plane in a gliding descent. Glancing through a side window Boyd saw the tree tops and instantly knew that the aircraft was dangerously low. He straddled the drafty opening. The wind noise made it nearly impossible to hear. The plane was now barely 300 feet from the ground - far too low for a safe jump. It was, in fact, an invitation for a crippling if not fatal fall. Boyd looked up and saw Burke sitting in the tail of the aircraft trying to buckle his parachute harness. His face and hands - like Boyd's - were already blistering from the heat. Burke had one leg harness buckled. Boyd had neither his chest or leg harness fastened. The machine gunner looked up at Boyd and said, "Help me."

As Boyd stood over the small opening in the tail of the burning B-25, his parachute hanging unbuckled and the heat now scorching the back of the plane, he heard a voice from within say, "Jump now John or you'll never jump." The Kentuckian crossed his arms, grabbed the rip cord, closed his legs and disappeared through the opening.

Technical Sergeant John W. Boyd survived that punishing jump only to be captured by the Japanese and held as a prisoner of war for 21 months in the notorious Rangoon Prison Camp in Rangoon, Burma. A highly-decorated veteran, among other honors Boyd received the Distinguished Flying Cross, Air Medal, Purple Heart, POW Medal. This is his story and that of the men with whom he shared the sufferings, torture, hope, triumphs and eventual allied victory in Rangoon, the China-Burma-India Theater and the Second World War. Their lives - and deaths - will forever be entwined with John Boyd's life and this story.

Gary Garth

Chapter 1

From Kentucky to Karachi

I was born in Graves County, Kentucky, December 12, 1918 to Albert and Zilla Boyd. I later had two sisters, Juanita and Martha. My family moved to Mayfield, Kentucky in 1923. Father was in the trucking business and mother worked in a clothing factory.

Growing up during the depression was an education within itself. We had few material goods, but with the exception of a few elite families in the community, were no different from anyone else. We created our own entertainment, and I have many precious memories from these times.

In the spring of 1941, after graduating from Mayfield High School, I was working as a soda "jerk" at Evan's Rexall Drug Store in Mayfield. This was the popular gathering place for Mayfield's young people. Mr. Bob Wyatt and his wife Francis owned the drug store and were two of the nicest people I've ever had the pleasure of knowing. It was truly a different time and place from today. Sodas were five cents, milk shakes were ten cents and sandwiches ten and fifteen cents. We also served a plate lunch that included a ham sandwich, potato salad, fruit and a fountain soda - all for 25 cents. Given the food the employees ate and the food we wasted I don't know how Mr. Wyatt made a profit. He had the patience of Job.

John Boyd, age 8.

I had no way of knowing it at the time but the memory of this town and the good people who lived there would be a source of strength for me during some of the things I would experience in Burma.

I was an average high school athlete and during the depression years, sports was one of the things that probably kept me going to school. Our teachers and coaches were dedicated people, teaching not only reading, writing and arithmetic, but also principals and values of life.

Europe was already embroiled in the Second World War. The United States military draft had started and the winds of war seemingly grew louder each day. Several of my high school friends

L-R: *John Boyd, Lester Smith, and Charles Clampett: 1937 Mayfield High Football Team.*

had volunteered for military service and it looked as though the United States would become involved in the war. If we did, I, like so many of my friends in Mayfield and other young people around the country, was determined to go and do my part. Johnny Bryan, Dalton Boyd, Dick Stubblefield, Edgar Smith, Nolan Russell and several of my friends had already joined the Air Force. I knew I had to go.

On June 8, 1941, a cousin, John Kennedy, was traveling to St. Louis, Missouri to pick up his wife Jean who had been visiting friends in South Dakota. I caught a ride with John to St. Louis and the next morning went to the downtown federal building and enlisted in the United States Army Air Corps.

I was sent to Jefferson Barracks, Missouri for basic training. After six weeks I was shipped to Scott Field, Illinois for training as a radio technician. Twenty-three years later, after serving in Asia, Europe and the United States, I retired from the military as the photographic supervisor at Scott Air Force Base.

During the summer of 1941 while in radio school we would frequently have our weekends free. My hometown of Mayfield, Kentucky was only about 190 miles from Scott Field so I would often hitchhike home on Saturday then hitchhike back to the base on Sunday. Sometimes I would do this alone. Other times I would go with friends.

On one occasion I and two other soldiers caught a ride not far from the base. A civilian and a soldier in a new fuel-injected Studabaker stopped. The civilian was driving. He said, "Get in soldiers. I need something to hold down the back end of this car." We later learned that the other soldier was the driver's brother, and he, too, was stationed at Scott Field. They were going to Memphis, Tennessee to pick up their mother and bring her back to St. Louis.

We were in for a wild ride. The top speed on the speedometer was 120 miles per hour. We came down Highway 3 from Chester, Illinois on a long open stretch of road. In those days these were all two lane highways. As we roared down the hill the speedometer reached 115; maybe faster. The three of us in the back were on the edge of our seat. As we approached the bottom of the hill a man pulled out in front of us on a tractor. The driver never flinched. He never checked his speed. He didn't touch his brakes. He just eased right around this farmer. As we looked back through the back window the man was just sitting on his tractor shaking his head.

When he stopped at Arlington, Kentucky to let me out we had driven 180 miles in two hours, and we had stopped one time for gas. When I got back to Scott Field I learned that he made the trip to Memphis and back safely. I found out later that this guy was a race car driver. One thing was certain, he certainly was a good driver. This was just one of my many experiences hitchhiking from Scott Field, Illinois to Mayfield, Kentucky during the summer of 1941.

On December 7, 1941 a few friends and I were enjoying weekend passes in St. Louis. Dalton Boyd, Ted Kennedy, Charles Libscomb and

John Boyd and Charley Hawkins- Soda Jerks, Evans Drug Store.

Albert and Zilla Boyd with their son, February 1942.

I had been in the city all day Saturday and had spent the night in Forest Park at a place called "tent city," which had been prepared for soldiers on weekend leave in St. Louis.

About 11 a.m. Sunday morning we were in a downtown restaurant near Sixth and Market Streets. A radio was on and the announcer was giving a report about the bombing at Pearl Harbor. Everyone became highly excited about it and started asking, "Could this really be true?" We thought no country would be stupid enough to attack the United States. Little did we know how inferior the United States was to the Japanese military at this time. In a little more than six months I would witness this first hand.

We were up most of the night going from place to place catching the news wherever we could. The radio reports were asking that all military men report to their bases immediately. We heard the requests but knew that when we got back on base that it would be a long time before we could get off again. So we didn't return to Scott Field until around 2 a.m.

The 30-week radio course was shortened to 22 weeks to fill the sudden need for radio operators. I graduated on February 3, 1942. The classes that only had a couple of weeks to go before the war started were shipped out before they had a chance to graduate. Some of these men were sent to the China-Burma-India Theater. Others went to Australia.

After graduation from radio school and a few days at home I was assigned to a B-26 bomber group in Jackson, Mississippi. It was here that volunteers were taken for the combat crews. I immediately volunteered for flying status.

The squadrons were organized before we had aircraft to fly. We started flying B-18s and anything else that would get off the ground. A few weeks later a few B-26 bombers began to arrive and by April 1 our flight group had moved to Columbia, South Carolina. At night I would lie in my bunk and listen to radio reports coming from the Philippines about how the allies were putting up a good fight but they couldn't

Evan's Drug Store on the far right on the corner of 7th and Broadway, Mayfield.

hold out much longer. I then made up my mind that I would go overseas; and the sooner, the better.

We had been in South Carolina about three weeks when the communications section chief came in and asked for three volunteers to go overseas. I and two other men quickly volunteered. We didn't know where we were going, but we knew they were forming two squadrons for an overseas base.

They turned out to be the 22nd and the 11th bomb squadrons of the 341st Bomb Group. The destinations were India and China. I was assigned to the 22nd Squadron with Lieutenant Robert "Alabama Bob" Puckett as the commanding officer, Lieutenant Zed Barns as the adjunct and Sergeant Thomas R. Pratt as the first sergeant. All were experienced men.

Most of the men who formed the 22nd squadron came from the 17th bomb group, Pendleton Field, Washington. This was the B-25 bomb group from which the crews and the planes were selected for the famous Doolittle Tokyo Raid. We did not know this at the time, however, and were soon sailing aboard the *USS Mariposa*, a former luxury liner that normally made the trip from California to Hawaii. We boarded the *Mariposa* on May 25, 1942; destination unknown. We were on this ship for 60 days and by the end of the journey all the airmen thought they were sailors.

We left Charleston with about 10,000 troops on the *Mariposa*. We had two meals a day and sometimes an apple in the afternoon. We were fed so much mutton that no one ever wanted to see another sheep. Later, though, in the Japanese prison camp, I often longed for a plate of that mutton.

I had never fired a machine gun but a merchant marine and I were assigned to man a turret armed with two 50 caliber, water-cooled machine guns. We welcomed the assignment because it let us get on deck for some fresh air. They had us stacked three bunks deep all over the ship. The hold was hot and crowded.

We left South Carolina and sailed across the Atlantic to Freetown, North Africa where we docked for a day and a night. We then sailed around Capetown, South Africa and through the Indian Ocean to Karachi, India. We had traveled about 17,000 miles escorted by the battleship *Texas*, two cruisers and some submarine chasers. At one point during the trip the convoy spotted a submarine and supposedly sank it. We were forced to travel the long Atlantic route because Japan had control of the Pacific.

The *Mariposa* was barely out of the South Carolina harbor before a blanket was laid on the floor and the gambling began. In a couple of weeks a few men had most of the money. When we reached Capetown we stopped to refuel and the commanding officer said we could all go ashore. This was great news except that most us were broke. A few men who had money pooled their funds and loaned the squadron some cash so we would have some money while ashore. It amounted to about $10 each, which was a good deal of money in those days. When we received our first payday after we arrived in India the money was paid back.

After three days in Capetown we started the final leg of our journey northward through the Indian Ocean to Karachi, India.

USS Mariposa.

Chapter 2

Chennault and the AVG

We arrived in Karachi, India on July 25, 1942 after being at sea for 60 days. It had only been about six months since the attack on Pearl Harbor and the United States was short on air power. There were about eight American bombers and just a few American fighters in this entire China-Burma-India Theater at this time.

The American Volunteer Group - the AVG "Flying Tigers" - had disbanded on July 4, 1942. The AVG was a collection of American civilian pilots who had been released from the United States Army, Navy and Marine Air Corps in order to fly for China against the Japanese. Although the group was small and always - always - outnumbered by the Japanese they had mettle, muscle and grit with a leader to match. The AVG operated under the command of retired Army Captain Claire Lee Chennault.

This operation was made possible through a secret arrangement between President Franklin D. Roosevelt, Captain Chennault and Generalissimo Chaing Kai-Shek. It was probably one of the largest covert military operations in U. S. history, and it was a true turning point early in the war. The AVG was the only American air power in the entire China-Burma-India Theater when the United States entered the war in December 1941.

Chennault had been forced into retirement by the Army Air Corps as a captain in June 1937. He went to China where he flew with and trained Chinese pilots until April 1941 when he returned to the United States for a visit to Washington D. C. Here he made arrangements with President Roosevelt for China to receive 100 obsolete P-40 fighter planes and then secured volunteer pilots from

Chin Hills, Burma.

the armed services to go to China as civilians and fly for the Chinese. President Roosevelt made arrangements so that all the men who wanted to volunteer would be released from their military service. For their services the men received a salary of $700 per month plus $500 for each enemy plane shot down. The pilots began arriving in Burma in July 1941.

The operation was risky, and the crews traveled to Burma by ship. They traveled on bogus passports masquerading as salesmen, business-men, ball players and men of other professions. They trained at Toungoo, a Burmese city about 100 miles north of Rangoon.

Chennault was a brilliant military strategist. He thoroughly under-stood both the strengths and limitation of the Japanese premier fight-ing plane - the Zero. Chennault refused to allow his pilots to engage in dogfights with the Zero. The reason for this was simple: he knew the Americans would most likely lose. This had nothing to do with his faith in the skill or courage of the American pilots - he knew that was unequaled. But he also understood that the Japanese Zero could easily out maneuver the older, heavier American P-40.

However, Chennault devised a strategy for fighting the Zero which worked repeatedly. He instructed his pilots to approach the Zero from above, dive on it, then fly away because the faster P-40 could easily escape the nimble but slower Japanese plane. Chennault reportedly told his pilots: "He who hits and runs away lives to hit another day."

Many stories are told about Claire Chennault. One shared by his flight engineer goes like this:

General Brady flew from India to China to see General Chennault. Brady landed and pulled up beside a DC-3. The DC-3 crew was lying in the shade under the wing of the air-craft. When General Brady got out of his aircraft the DC-3 crew leaned forward, looked at him, then lay back down. The general stormed into Chennault's office. "Whose DC-3 is parked on the ramp!" he demanded. "I parked beside it and not one man called attention or saluted." Chennault calmly replied, "General Brady, that's my crew and that's my aircraft. They don't salute me when I go out there, and I know they're not going to salute you when you go out there." Chennault went on to inform his fellow officer, "If you don't like the way I run this business in China get in your airplane and go back to In-dia."

On Christmas Day 1941 the Japanese appeared over Rangoon, Burma with 70 bombers and 40 fighters. Thirteen AVG and 12 RAF fighters went up to meet them. In a brutal three hour battle the AVG lost one plane. They shot down 40 Japanese aircraft.

During the week after Christmas the AVG shot down 63 Japanese and only lost two aircraft. The AVG kill ratio was nothing short of astounding and it proved not to be a fluke. By March 1942 the American volunteers had destroyed 299 planes while losing only seven.

The AVG's biggest single contribution to the war, however, came on May 7, 1942 when the famed Japanese 56th Red Dragon Division was on the Burma Road and poised the mile-deep Salween River gorge on the Burma-China border. The Chinese blew the bridge but the Japanese quickly constructed a pontoon bridge, which was quickly spotted by the AVG.

Eight AVG planes again blew the bridge. Then the AVG, along with the Chinese army, killed 4,500 advancing Japanese. This stemmed the tide of the 56th Red Dragon Division's drive into China. It was an early turning point in the China-Burma-India Theater because the Japanese never again tried to cross the Salween River into China. Had they been successful in moving into China they would have had a clear advance to Kunming. All of northern China almost certainly would have fallen under Japanese control. The allies then would not have a base from which to operate in China. Essentially, the AVG was responsible for keeping the Japanese out of China.

On February 25, 1942 the Japanese sent 166 planes to Kunming. Nine AVG aircraft shot down 21 confirmed and 30 probable Japanese planes without a single loss. The next day the Japanese sent another 200 planes to Kunming. This time six AVG pilots downed 18 enemy planes without a single loss.

The AVG never had more than 55 planes available and never more than 24 in the air at one time.

In July 1942 Chennault was called back to active duty as a brigadier general and in March 1943 was promoted to major general.

The 14th Air Force under Major General Chennault was credited with 2,315 aircraft destroyed with an additional 773 "probable" destroyed between July 1942 and May 1945. They had killed approximately 1,500 Japanese pilots, navigators, bombardiers and gunners; destroyed 2,135 merchant ships; 817 bridges, 1,225 locomotives and killed 59,454 Japanese troops.

After the war the Japanese records revealed that the AVG was thought to have had 1,500 planes. The actual number was 55.

Claire Chennault was a great general who was loved and respected by both enlisted men and officers. However, he did not get along well with some other commanders, including many in Washington D. C.

After fighting the Japanese for eight years, and just weeks before the Japanese surrender on the *USS Missouri*, General Chennault was again forced into retirement. If ever any man deserved to stand with the allied forces on the deck of the *Missouri* when Japan surrendered it was Major General Claire L. Chennault, but his contributions went unrecognized at the surrender.

Through a special act of Congress, which was signed by President Dwight D. Eisenhower, General Chennault was advanced to the rank of lieutenant general a few days before his death on July 27, 1958.

Chapter 3
India

By October 1, 1942 the 22nd bomb squadron had settled in Karachi, India while the 11th bomb squadron had gone to China. By this time Colonel Jimmy Doolittle had also lead the famous "Doolittle Raid" on Tokyo.

Doolittle and his crew had launched their attack from the aircraft carrier *Hornet*. While the mission did little physical damage it shocked the Japanese and provided the United States with a badly-needed morale boost.

One plane from the Doolittle Raid landed safely in Russian territory but the other crews were forced to bail out when their planes ran out of fuel. Doolittle and most of his crew walked safely out of the jungles but two crews were captured by the Japanese. The Japanese shot the two pilots and one gunner leaving five surviving members from the 10 men who had to crash land along the coast of China (two were killed in the crash).

After Colonel Doolittle reached Kunming he took his crews that had reached that Chinese city and returned to the United States. When his remaining crews arrived in Kunming they were assigned to the 22nd, 11th and 491st bomb squadrons of the 341st Bomb Group. They remained active in the China-Burma-India Theater for about a year.

I and flight engineer George "Danny" Danfield, who sailed to India with me on the *Mariposa*, were promoted to staff sergeants and assigned to the same flight crew. Some of the men from the Doolittle crews were assigned to our squadron. They were Captain Thadd Blanton, pilot; and Captain Edward McLeroy, pilot; Captain Robert "Bob" Gray, pilot; Sergeants Jones and Bushwall and Sergeant Fred Braumer, who was the bombardier on General Doolittle's plane. A few other men from the Doolittle bunch were assigned to the 22nd squadron.

By late October 1942 crews were being assigned and everyone was excited about who they would get as a pilot. Naturally, each man wanted the best pilot and after assignments were announced each man thought he had the best pilot. I was in the barracks laying on my bunk trying to keep cool when Danfield came running in and said, "Boyd, they've just posted the crews. Guess who our pilot is?" I said I didn't know. Danfield shouted, "It's Captain Bob Gray."

I didn't know Bob Gray from John Doe, but Danfield had come from the 17th bomb group at Pendleton Field, Washington, and this was the same group from which Doolittle's Tokyo crews were picked.

He knew Captain Gray and was quick to announce that he was the best pilot in the 17th Bomb Group. He was also one of the wildest and most exciting pilots in the Air Force.

There were a lot of stories told about Captain Gray. One involved him making - or trying to make - an unscheduled stop while flying cross country on the way to the *USS Hornet*, for the Doolittle mission. The story goes like this:

Gray's father was said to have been a sheriff in a small town in Texas. Captain Gray called his father and told him what time he would be at his home town and asked if his father would go rope off the highway just outside the town. He would land his B-25, and have a short visit with them. According to the story Gray made three attempts to put the bomber down on the Texas highway but wasn't able to do so.

When crew assignments were made in October 1942 our crew included Captain Robert "Bob" Gray, pilot; Captain Thadd Blanton, copilot; Lieutenant Alex Porter, navigator; Lieutenant Joe Cunningham, bombardier; Staff Sergeant George Danfield, engineer; and Staff Sergeant John Boyd, radio operator.

On October 23, 1942, the 22nd was scheduled for its first mission - a raid on Hong Kong and Canton, China. At that time our bombers had not been over either Hong Kong or Canton. However, the AVG fighters had been to these cities and General Chennault and General Caleb V. Haynes thought it was time to show the Japanese that they could be hit by American bombers. They came from the 11th squadron, which was already at Kunming, and our 22nd squadron, which was in Karachi, India. The 22nd squadron flew across India to Dinjan and from there "cross the hump" (the Himalayas) into China. From there we went on to Kunming, loaded up with bombs and fuel, then on October 25 hit Hong Kong. We then came back to Kweilin,

John Boyd (far left) and engineer George Danfield (far right) with their ground crew in 1943.

Flying over the Chin Hills, Burma.

China, which was an advance base that one week would be in the hands of the Chinese then the next week might be in the hands of the Japanese. There we loaded up again with bombs and fuel and bomb Canton, China.

That completed, we returned to Kunming, then back to Karachi, India - a round trip of approximately 5,600 miles. General Haynes lead the bombers while Colonel Robert Scott and Major Tex Hill were scheduled to lead the fighter escorts to Hong Kong. This was the mission Colonel Scott wrote about in his book *God is My Co-Pilot.*

I didn't make the flight. Captain Gray received word that his Tokyo crew was at Dinjan, and he requested and received permission to pick them up there and take them on this mission. So the rest of the crew stayed behind. Lieutenant Cunningham was re-assigned to another crew. They were shot down on this mission after completing a special assignment.

The air strip at Karachi was a temporary makeshift affair complete with a wooden control tower about 20 feet high. In it was a generator-powered command radio set. Our crew went out the next morning to watch the planes take off, disappointed and a little mad that we had been left behind. Captain Gray had a passenger riding with him to Dinjan who was taking his first airplane ride. We watched Gray make a normal take off. About the time we thought he was on his way to Dinjan he made a circle and headed for the control tower, flying very close to the ground. Just before he got to the tower he lifted the plane. The prop wash rocked the tower so hard the two men in it landed flat on their bellies. He then lifted the plane into a steep climb and soon disappeared from sight.

Captain Gray picked-up his regular crew in Dinjan and started across the hump to China. According to Captain Blanton, the last they heard from Gray was that he had one engine out but was going to try to cross the hump anyway. They never made it to Kunming.

This was the first of several times when fate would fall into my favor.

When the planes from the 22nd squadron reached Kunming, they joined the B-25s from the 11th squadron at Yunnan, which was near Kunming. On the morning of October 25, 1942 ten B-25 bombers and seven P-40 fighters took off for Hong Kong. The bombers were lead by General Haynes with Major Morgan as the lead bombardier. The formation flew in two V-flights of three planes each and one box of four in the rear. In aircraft number 59, a B-25B (one of the oldest and slowest aircraft in the squadron but one that had been in the theater several months and had a lot of combat time) Lieutenant Aller was the pilot, Lieutenant Joe Cunningham was the bombardier and Rusty Webb

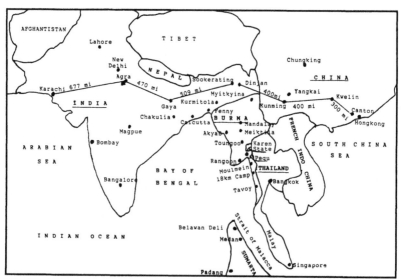

The 22nd Bomb Squadron's first mission as a squadron on October 25, 1942. The flight was from Karachi, India for a raid on Hong Kong and Canton, China and back to Karachi, This was approximately a 5,500 mile mission.

John Boyd's original crew: standing L-R: Capt. Thad Bianton, Lt. John Lemich, Lt. McGraw, Lt. Joseph W. Cunningham, Kneeling: S/Sgt. George Danfield, T/Sgt. John Boyd.

was the top turret gunner. Cunningham and Sergeant Webb each downed a Japanese fighter that day.

The target was the docks in the Hong Kong harbor. At the flight briefing, General Chennault told Cunningham and Aller that there was a transport sitting in the harbor away from the docks. The general asked Cunningham if he could hit the transport if Aller would drop out of the formation and get to the ship. Cunningham said he could. Aller was flying "tail end Charlie" so he easily dropped out of the formation. Joe Cunningham did hit and destroy the transport, for which he would receive the Silver Star.

When Aller came off the target he was met with heavy anti-aircraft fire and the plane was jumped by more than 30 Zeros. The old B-25 lost one engine to enemy fire and dropped behind in the formation. Aller and his crew were forced to bail out.

The crew re-grouped on the ground and attempted to return to friendly territory, but Aller had been shot in the foot and was badly in need of medical attention. When the group stopped to rest Cunningham and co-pilot Wilbur Marcus went to find some water. As they returned, they heard Japanese voices, so they stopped and took cover. Their crew had been captured. Powerless to help, the two men hid until the Japanese left with their crew mates. After several days, Cunningham and Marcus did return to friendly territory. The two returned to the 22nd bomb squadron and Cunningham joined our crew and flew with us until he and Captain Blanton returned to the United States in July 1943. Lieutenant Marcus was killed a few months later in an aircraft accident.

After they bombed the docks at Hong Kong that day, the B-25s went to Kweilin where they re-fueled and re-armed. That night six planes went to Canton for a successful raid before returning to Kunming. Then it was on to Karachi.

The mission was a tremendous success. We lost only one bomber, Lieutenant Aller's crew, and one fighter, although the fighter pilot returned safely to Kunming. The bombers and fighters destroyed 27 enemy aircraft, they bombed the docks and sunk a transport. Perhaps most importantly the Japanese now knew we could hit Hong Kong and Canton with authority.

As soon as the B-25 got back to Karachi the 22nd squadron made preparations to move to Chakulia, India which was about 100 miles west of Calcutta. It was from here that we would start regular bombing missions over Burma.

Chapter 4

Haynes

General Caleb V. Haynes was commander of the India Air Task Force. He liked the B-25 aircraft and our 22nd squadron would on occasion furnish him with a crew and plane to fly around India and inspect the bases. Hugh Crumpler, a writer for the *Ex-CBI Roundup* wrote of Haynes:

(He) reached Dinjan, in the spring of 1942, and was one of the first officers to command the pioneer units that established The Hump route to China. Haynes, one of America's most experienced fighter and bomber pilots, was characterized as follows by General Claire Chennault: 'Caleb V. Haynes looked like a gorilla and flew like an angel.'

In the C-B-I (China-Burma-India) Theater, Haynes commanded the Indian Air Task Force and three heavy bomb groups of the 14th Air Force in China. They were the 7th, 12th, and 308th Bomb Groups. Haynes and his crew once took on a Japanese fighter while flying a DC-3 on The Hump run. They fired Tommy guns and Colt 45s and just about anything they had at the fighter. Apparently the Japanese thought he had run into some kind of a buzz saw or new kind of a heavily-armed American aircraft because he left the scene at top speed.

...Caleb Haynes was a pilot's pilot. And he was made of the right stuff of heroes. In his lifetime, though, fate decreed that he would never receive the recognition and the public acclaim that came to many lesser men. Only other pioneer aviators fully recognized the genius of Caleb Haynes.

Crumpler pointed to the famous Doolittle raid on Tokyo as an example of the twisted fate that sometimes followed Haynes.

The Tokyo raid was originally planned to start from two take off points. The plan called for Doolittle to lead a group of B-25s from the carrier Hornet.

The other arm of the first Tokyo raid was to have come from the Philippines. It was to have been a group of B-17s, lead by Caleb Haynes. So, as first planned, the bombing attacks on Tokyo were to have come from two different directions lead by two of Americas greatest fliers: Caleb Haynes from the Philippines and Jimmy Doolittle from an aircraft carrier in the Pacific Ocean. What went wrong with this plan?

The Chinese army went wrong. Caleb Haynes and his B-17s, because of the distance to Tokyo from the Philippines, were to have landed in east China after the bombing of Tokyo. But the Chinese army had retreated in the face of Japanese attacks. Their retreat allowed the Japanese to overrun the eastern China airstrips that would have been used by (Haynes) B-17s. Haynes would have had no place to land after the raid so the B-17 arm of the two prong raid was canceled. Haynes' group never left the Philippines.

Jimmy Doolittle's Tokyo raid was a smashing psychological success, one of the first morale boosters for America in the war against Japan. Doolittle and his raid survivors were instant national heroes. And, deservedly so.

Most of the men in Caleb Haynes' group never knew it, but except for the fickle finger of fate they would have bombed Tokyo simultaneously with Doolittle raiders.

When the group was reassigned to India, Haynes had become commander of an unusual miniature air force. His new group consisted of seven B-17s, seven C-47s and Haynes' own command aircraft, one B-24 Liberator.

In the relative obscurity of the China-Burma-India Theater, and in the world's worst flying conditions, Caleb Haynes continued the career that made him one of the all time legends of the air.

He was, as Papa Tiger Claire Chennault said, a man 'who looked like a gorilla and flew like an angel.'

His legend grew.

He was half man, half propeller

He was Paul Bunyan in goggles and helmet.

He was the all-time pilot's pilot.

That was Caleb Haynes known by other airmen. But not by the general public.

Riding along in the B-24D as a passenger when Haynes lead his flight group to Karachi, was Colonel Marian C. Cooper, a motion picture producer (he wrote and produced the movie *King Kong*). He was to serve as Haynes' deputy, and he later served with the 14th Air Force.

General Haynes was as responsible as any officer for the development of the B-17 flying fortress. He flew B-18s in the early days across the ice cap. He flew in open cockpits. He made the long range intercep-tor flights in 1937-38 that provided information for aircraft to later locate and bomb enemy ships. In July 1941, Haynes was selected to pioneer the transatlantic service of the Army and Air Force. Flying a B-24 he established the Atlantic route that would be used throughout World War II.

Haynes was again called upon when it became necessary to open a south Atlantic route through Florida, Brazil and West Africa to the Middle East. Again flying a B-24, Haynes established the route. On the first survey flight his co-pilot was Major Curtis E. LeMay. Many of the flight officers who went on to become distinguished commanders dur-ing World War II - like Curtis LeMay - at some point during their ca-reers flew as Caleb Haynes' co-pilot.

General Haynes had a sense of humor but he had a long memory, particularly where the Japanese were concerned. He had come to China to lead General Chennault's bombers when Tokyo Rose, who followed Haynes' career, referred to him as, "The old broken down transport pilot."

When Haynes was made commander of the Indian Air Task Force, Tokyo Rose announced on the radio that "we don't have anything to worry about over here any more. They've made that old broken down transport pilot commander in chief." That made Haynes so mad he could have torn the Japanese to pieces with his bare hands. After all, he had been a pursuit pilot for many years, and for the past 10 years he had been the dean of America's four engine bomber pilots. The records he had set with the B-15s had made history and were an inspiration to everyone in the Army Air Corps. The Japanese knew how to get under his skin. In the end,

General Haynes decorating Doolittle Tokyo crew members, January 1943.

though, it worked against them. He didn't have a plane that would deliver a bomb load so he loaded a DC-3 with some 100 lb. fragment bombs then took some soldiers with him to throw the bombs out of the aircraft. He returned the next day and dropped thousands of leaflets that he had printed announcing the previous days bomb load was, "COMPLIMENTS OF THE OLD BROKEN DOWN TRANSPORT PILOT."

Then in October 1942 came the time for him to lead the first raids on Hong Kong and Canton. Quite often then, after the October 1942 raid when Haynes' bombers would deliver a load, they would also throw out some the same leaflets.

On November 23, 1942 while our squadron was preparing to move from Karachi to Chakulia, Captain Blanton, Lieutenant William Nau, Lieutenant Alex Porter, Sergeant Danfield and I were selected to fly with General Haynes. We were not sent to fly him around the country. Haynes did his own flying. We just flew with him. We made several flights around India until around the second week of January 1943 when we returned to the squadron at Chakulia. General Haynes was 48 years old at this time and one of the best officers I've ever known. He put you at ease whenever you were around him. However, everyone had great respect for him as an officer and as a person. He was not a desk general but a field and operations commander who believed in getting the job done. He didn't ask a man to do anything he wouldn't do himself. This was an important lesson I learned from General Haynes. It was very useful to me during my years in public office and in the real estate business.

On one occasion when Sergeant Danfield and I were at the aircraft doing the daily inspection, we saw a staff car approaching. General Haynes got out, walked up to Danfield and said, "Son, we spotted a cruiser in the Bay of Bengal. Is this aircraft ready to go?"

Danfield replied, "Yes sir. We're ready to go."

General Haynes then said, "Well, you don't have any bombs."

Danfield said, "We can get some from the British." (They were positioned at the same base.)

Haynes just grinned and said, "I just wanted to check and see if you were ready to go." He then stayed around that day and chatted with us for awhile.

Major General Caleb V. Haynes died at his home in Carmel, California, at age 71 on April 5, 1966, a day when American aviation and the China-Burma-India Theater lost one of the greatest fliers of all time.

Chapter 5

"Shoot Them in the Morning."

From January to August 1943 our missions were all directed over Burma. The targets were railroad yards, bridges and air fields. We were bombing from an altitude of 10,000 to 12,000 feet. One of our hottest targets was the Myitnge Bridge just south of Mandalay, Burma, over the Irrawaddy River. Each time we would think we had knocked it out. But then the next day the P-38 reconnaissance would fly over and take pictures and show it to still be intact. After I was captured I found that the Japanese were stringing it back together with bamboo minutes after the raid was over. They had a good reason for doing this. The bridge provided an excellent position for Japanese anti-aircraft fire. Although the bamboo bridge was useless it kept the bombers coming back, subjecting them to deadly anti-aircraft fire and causing the allies to waste bombs on a target that was already destroyed.

In July 1943 we began practicing "skip bombing;" a maneuver during which the pilot brought the plane down to tree top level, released the bomb, then pull up before it exploded.

On August 3 Lieutenant Charles McCook's crew, along with one other B-25 from the 22nd squadron met a crew from the 490th squadron at the 490th's base in Kurmitola, India. From there the three planes left to make an experimental skip bombing run on a dam near Meiktila,

Officers of the 22nd Bomb Squadron, 1942.

Burma. Sergeant Wood, the regular radio man on McCook's crew, was on a pass to Calcutta. Wood had previously taken my place when I was on pass, so I agreed to take his place on this mission.

My regular pilot and bombardier had returned to the United States in July. In August 1943 my crew included Lieutenant John Lemich, pilot; Flight Officer John Weaver, co-pilot; Lieutenant Max Greenstein, bombardier, Sergeant Danfield, engi-

Sgts. George Danfield, John Boyd, and Thomas Pratt display remnants of a turkey buzzard that burst the plexiglass during a mission, slid through the bombardiers tunnel, hit the bomb bay door release, and opened the bomb bay doors.

neer; and myself, radio operator. We did not have an assigned gunner.

After capture I thought it would have been better if I had stayed with my regular crew. However, my flying with McCook and being shot down ultimately saved my life because on September 10 my regular crew was killed in a mission over Burma. If I hadn't been with McCook's crew on August 3, I would almost certainly have been in that fatal September crash.

On our way out to the flight line the morning of August 3, I saw Sergeant Wood. My first thought was to tell him he had a mission. But since he had flown for me while I was on leave I thought it best that I take his place. The flight crew for this mission included Lieutenant Charles McCook, pilot; Lieutenant Nathaniel L. Hightower, co-pilot; Lieutenant Henry J. Carlin, navigator; Sergeant John E. Leisure, gunner and engineer, Sergeant Sidney Burke, gunner and me, Technical Sergeant John W. Boyd, radio operator and gunner.

When we got to the flight line and ran the engines for the flight check we discovered a pressure drop in the left engine. McCook told the other crew to go on to Kurmitola, and that we would catch up with them. We were delayed about an hour and by the time we got to Kurmitola the 22nd and the 490th crews had already had their lunch and were coming to the flight line from their target briefing.

The target was the dam on the Irrawaddy River at Meiktila, which was one of the Japanese headquarter sites in central Burma. When the

British army drove through Burma in April 1945, the dam was the site of a major battle in which approximately 6,000 Japanese were killed.

We were instructed to follow the other two planes on the target approach. On the final run each plane would drop to near treetop level and then go straight in. We would go in one plane behind the other - first in, first out. Our aircraft was to be the last one in and the last one out.

As we approached the bomb target, McCook brought the B-25 down to 1,500 feet. Sergeant Burke, in the top turret, asked the pilot if he could strafe the ground cover when we came down to start the target run. Lieutenant McCook said, "Yes, that would be OK."

McCook came down to near treetop level and Burke began strafing the area. Before we reached a target, I always found time to ask God to watch over and protect us. This time though, I had not remembered to do this. Just as we started the run I remembered a letter that I had received from Mrs. McNeely, one of my childhood Sunday School teachers. The words flashed through my mind: "Ask of Him for He is there." So I quickly prayed "Lord watch over us and protect us."

Ground guns guarded the approach to the target. The first plane had probably surprised the Japanese, and the second plane probably helped the gunners to get their distance. We must have flown almost

Indians extending the runways at Chakulia, India early 1943 to get ready for the B-29s which took the base over in 1944.

directly over one of the gun positions. I sat on the floor with my back against the bombardier compartment. When we came down on the target I could see the tracers blinking at us from both sides. As radio operator I also had charge of two 30 caliber machine guns in the belly of the plane.

Back row L-R: T/Sgt Wood, S/Sgt Glen Bowen, T/Sgt. Vanmarter, unknown, S/Sgt. Shipley, S/Sgt. Jackson, S/Sgt. George Danfield, unknown. Front row L-R: T/Sgt Leon "Nick" Weber, Sgt. John Leisure (below Weber), S/Sgt Bert Jordan, S/Sgt Arthur "Art" Dewalt, unknown.

Our parachutes were the long "seat type" chutes that older veterans will remember. When the chute was strapped to your back it hung down below the waist and provided a foam rubber seat. This is what the pilot sat on. To secure the chute, straps came up over the shoulders and buckled at the chest. There were also two leg straps to secure the bottom of the chute. When the parachute was not being worn it was folded and buckled together into a tight package.

From the radio operator's position you could see all the way to the tail of the airplane but not forward toward the cockpit. Access to cockpit was made through a crawl space over the bomb bay compartment. This space was closed by a zippered canvas partition. The B-25s also had two small windows on each side of the aircraft behind the wing. While making a low run the man in the radio operator's position could see the treetops and the tracers from the blinking guns. From the air the muzzle blasts look like a light going on and off.

About halfway between the bomb bay and the tail was a two foot square opening in the floor of the aircraft. This served as a door to enter the plane. It was fitted with an emergency release which let it, and the ladder, drop free. This was the bail-out exit for the radio operator, gunner and engineer.

The correct bail out procedure was to sit on the floor of the airplane- facing the front of the plane, reach forward and grab the front of the opening, slide off the floor, hang for a second then release for a free fall. That was the textbook method.

From high altitude I could normally look through the gun hole in the bottom of the plane and see the bombs hit the target. But from treetop level and sliding the bombs into the target like we were doing today I couldn't see the bombs come out.

We were on the final run and the ground guns were blazing when suddenly we got hit just inside the bomb bay. It must have been an explosive shell of some type because it made a deafening noise and violently shook the aircraft.

McCook took the plane into a steep climb, but we immediately began to feel the heat from the fire inside the bomb bay. It was heating up fast. Sergeant Leisure was sitting on the waist guns behind the opening in the floor with his chute on. He immediately released the door in the floor of the plane. Leisure had bailed out once before and knew what to do. Sergeant Burke was in the turret, and neither he nor I had our chutes on. Burke couldn't wear his chute in the turret and I used mine as a seat cushion. I knew some men who had been shot in the bottom by ground fire, and since I sat on the floor of the plane, I sat on my chute because I would rather have had anti-aircraft fire in my parachute than in me.

Smoke was beginning to spread throughout the airplane and the heat was intense. The fire in the bomb bay had burned through the intercom wiring so communication with the cockpit was lost. The wind draft through the tail of a B-25 turned the fire into a blow torch. We reacted almost without thinking.

I punched Burke on the leg. When he looked down I motioned for him to get out of the turret. As he was getting out I unbuckled his chute and held it open while he slipped. By this time the plane may have been up to about 1,000 feet. Leisure motioned that he was going out. He dropped through the floor of the airplane, held for moment, released himself and was gone. We were high enough that Leisure said later that he was able to float for a while before he hit the ground.

I unbuckled my chute, shook it loose, slid my arms though the straps and started toward the back of the plane. As a passed the window I glanced out and saw the treetops. I knew then that we were very low. When I got to the back of the plane I was standing up, straddling the opening in the floor with a foot on each side. Sergeant Burke was sitting on a seat with his chest straps fastened. He also had one leg strap fastened and was trying to snap the other. His face and hands were blistered from the heat. He glanced up and said, "Help me." In that instant a voice flashed through my mind just as clear is if someone had spoken it. It said: "Jump now, John, or you'll never jump."

Without thinking, I closed my legs and fell through the door. I crossed my arms across my chest to hold the straps closed since the chute was not buckled. The instant my head cleared the door I pulled the rip cord.

* * *

The time difference between Mayfield, Kentucky and central Burma is about 10 hours. I was shot down around 2 p. m. on August 3, 1943. In Mayfield, Kentucky, about 4 a.m. that same day my father awoke, sat up in bed and said, "Wake up Zilla (that was my mother's name). I saw John falling through space surrounded by fire." My mother answered, "Lay down Albert and go back to sleep. You're dreaming. But my father was adamant about this disturbing sensation and awoke my sister and told her to make a note of the date. A few weeks later they got the message that I had been missing in action since August 3. This event was witnessed by my mother and two sisters. I still cannot explain it.

* * *

By the time I jumped, the plane must have been down to about 300 feet because we were in a landing approach glide. I knew the plane was low but had I known it was that low I certainly would not have jumped.

When the first chute opened I swung up, then just as I swung back down the main chute popped opened. It jerked my head back and my feet hit the ground. The impact knocked my knees back under my chin and my head went forward and - it's strange how you remember these things - when I stopped I was still sitting on the foam rubber seat of the parachute.

Behind me was a stand of hardwoods. There was also a strip of timber along the north side of a long open field. By the time I hit the ground and managed to raise my head McCook had brought the plane down along the side of the field and had made his first left bank and was going into his second left bank to come back up the field toward me for a belly landing. The B-25 was about 15 feet above the treetops. Both engines were running, and he was holding the plane steady for a perfect belly landing. Although smoke was billowing from the bomb bay he set it down smoothly. The moment it touched the ground clouds of smoke boiled up from the plane. By the time it stopped sliding everything was one big ball of black smoke. From my position to the point where McCook made his final turn was the distance of a short runway - maybe 3,000 feet. But it was far enough that I did not hear an explosion. Everything just went up in one big cloud of smoke.

B-25s from 22nd Bomb Squadron, 341st Bomb Group flying in box formation.

In the prison camp Leisure told me that as he was floating under his parachute, the last time he saw the aircraft smoke was coming from the bottom of the plane where the fire was burning in the bomb bay compartment. The aircraft had crossed over a field and was going over some woods at a very low altitude. He hadn't seen anyone else bail out. He was surprised when he saw me because he didn't think anyone could have made it out of the plane.

I have used a stop watch and retraced my actions to see how much time elapsed from when the plane was hit until I hit the ground. The best that I can determine is that it was 45 to 50 seconds that passed.

I tried to get up but felt a sharp pain in my lower abdomen and upper legs. My face and both hands were burned, with the left hand the most badly damaged. I saw two or three people running toward me. I first thought they might be Burmese natives. Then I saw more people coming up behind them. I thought, "If they are natives, I'll scare them off." When I fired a shot over their heads with my .45 caliber sidearm they hit the ground. But they got right up and continued toward me. I fired again. This time as they hit the ground they fired back with a .25 caliber pistol. The bullet was close enough I could hear it sing as went by. I can still tell by sound the difference between a .45 caliber and a .25 caliber pistol.

I could see they were wearing uniforms. The uniforms weren't as neat as the ones worn by American and British soldiers. I thought, "Maybe they're Burmese," and threw my pistol in front of me and raised my hands. Then they really came on a dead run. When they were about 50 yards away I could see that the first man had a rifle with a fixed bayonet, and he was on a bayonet charge. Fifty feet or so behind him was another soldier with the .25 caliber pistol. I found out later that he was a sergeant and the soldier with the rifle was a private. The sergeant was shouting "Demarti! Demarti! Demarti!" I didn't know what "demarti" meant, but I later learned that it means "halt" in Japanese. But this soldier didn't halt. He continued on a dead run. When he was about three feet away he turned slightly and rammed the bayonet into the ground only a couple of inches from my abdomen. It was a close call.

The sergeant had arrived and tried to push the soldier who had been on the bayonet charge to one side. The soldier with the rifle and bayonet was shouting and stomping his feet. He obviously wanted to kill me. A Japanese interrogator later asked, "Do you remember the soldier who tried to bayonet you?" I told him that I certainly did. The interrogator told me that he was a mean man but a good soldier. He said this soldier had killed many men. He didn't have to try and convince me. I believed him.

The Japanese tied my hands behind my back and began to pull me as I tried to walk. I had hit the ground so hard that I couldn't raise my feet without experiencing severe pain across the lower part of my abdomen. They pushed me to a waiting truck. An angry crowd of Burmese were hitting me with sticks and clubs and trying to reach me. They were as harsh as the Japanese. My hands were tied and were burned but one old man was picking at the burned flesh. The Burmese may have been angered because Sergeant Burke had strafed the area as we came in on the target.

Two Japanese joined me in the back of the truck. We traveled only a short distance before stopping where a couple more Japanese soldiers were standing with John Leisure. I was sure glad to see Leisure, and he was happy to see me because he didn't think any other members of the crew had survived the crash.

They threw him in the truck and took us to a small building that was being used as the guard house. A crowd gathered and an English-speaking Japanese officer soon appeared. The Japanese surrounding us were very excited. A Japanese sergeant gave my .45 caliber sidearm, which was still loaded, cocked and ready to fire, to one of his officers, who began waving it around. I would not have cared if he had pulled the trigger and killed a Japanese soldier, but he was pointing and waving the gun toward Leisure and I. I said, "The clip is in the gun," and pointed toward the pistol. He may have thought that I reaching for the gun because he smacked me on the side of the head. He then removed the clip.

A few minutes later the gunner who had shot us down arrived. He received hearty congratulations from the crowd.

An officer quieted the crowd then and Japanese began an interrogation. They wanted to know what kind of plane we were flying, our rank, and our position on the aircraft. I told him I was a technical sergeant radio operator and Leisure said that he was a sergeant and a flight engineer. The officer asked me if I was the one who had strafed the village, and I told him, "No. That was the gunner." They then began to untie Leisure's hands and feet. When I asked them to untie my hands and feet, they loosened my hands, but not my feet. This didn't make sense to me. Leisure was uninjured, and I was burned and hurt. But it may have been because I shot at them, or they may have thought I was grabbing at the gun.

They talked amongst themselves for a few minutes. The English-speaking officer was preparing to leave when the sergeant asked what they were to do with us. The officer turned, looked at us, and calmly replied, "Shoot them in the morning."

I don't know their true intentions. But Leisure and I believed they were going to kill us the next morning. The Japanese officer walked away. I looked at Leisure and said, "Did you hear what he said?"

"Yes."

"Then I guess this is it."

Leisure answered, "Yes."

They left us under guard tied and bound on the porch of the guard house. We didn't speak for a long time. The crowd began to leave and it looked like they were not even going to interrogate us. They were just going to shoot us in the morning.

I can't tell you what Leisure thought, but I thought it was all over. I had some close calls before, but they were over in a short time and usually occurred in the middle of heavy action when I really didn't have time to think about my survival. I simply reacted.

This time was different because I had all night to think about it my inevitable death.

Leisure and I remained silent most of the night, each left to his own thoughts I suppose. Neither of us enjoyed much sleep. We were waiting for the morning. The night seemed to pass quickly and the

Japanese came into the guard room every few hours. We would hear them rattling the rifle racks and talking.

After Japanese officers and the crowd left, the realization of what happened and what was about to happen began to settle in. The first thing I thought of was, "Well, it's all over." Then I asked myself how I got into this mess and if it was really worth it.

I had volunteered for combat duty and knew that I had not been required to come overseas when I did. I was pretty sure that I could have managed a non-combative job in the States. I also thought about this particular mission - I did not have to go.

I was only 24 years old - too young to die, I decided. Then I remembered some of my friends who had not lived to be 24. As I was thinking about these things I knew I had much to be thankful. But I still wanted to live longer.

Throughout the night, I imagined the future I would now miss. Who would I have married? Would I have had children? And would they have been boys or girls?

I thought about my squadron and the other two planes that were on the mission with us that day. I knew they were back in Chakulia now, probably wondering what had happened to us.

I thought about my family and friends back in Kentucky, and knew that they'd be getting the news very soon that I was missing in action. Only I wouldn't be missing. I would be dead.

And I thought, "Is all this worth it. What will it be like if we don't win this war?" We didn't start it. I knew that if the Japanese got what they wanted then our families; all the good people back in Mayfield; and all over the United States would suffer. I knew there were a lot of wicked people in the world, but then I thought for a minute and realized that there are a lot of good people, too.

"All this fighting and dying; we're doing this for all the good people," I thought A few months later in the prison camp and even 36 years later in 1979 when the crash came in the real estate business, I found this sentiment remained true: There are many good people in the world. And they're willing to help you.

I thought of all the people in my hometown who had an influence on my life; my parents, sisters, cousins and other relatives and the close family ties that we had. I thought of so many other people in my home town who had helped me. One was a high school English teacher, Mrs. Florence Wyman. I was probably the poorest English student she ever had, but her teaching went far beyond the books. She taught me about character and demonstrated the good things in life by how she took an interest in everyone. I thought of Mrs. McNeely and coach Ray Ross and J. P. Glasgow and Bob Wyatt and George Stone and so many of the others who had helped the young people in Mayfield to try and become good citizens.

I thought of these folks and knew we would win this war, but I also knew that no war can be won, and peace cannot be attained, until so many lives had been given. I thought that fate had determined that I would now be one of those lives.

Then I said to myself, "Yes, it was worth it."

I thought about the Japanese. They were wrong, but I knew that they believed they were right. Although I knew - absolutely knew - that we were right, I spent part of the night trying to accept the harsh fact that I had been selected to be one of the casualties of war.

I then remembered Christ on the cross when he said, "Forgive them Father for they know not what they do." And I thought, "If my Lord can do that for those who crucified him I certainly must do the same," and I prayed the same prayer, "Forgive them Lord for they know not what they do."

At dawn Leisure and I shook hands and said that it was very good to have known one another. I told Leisure that, given a choice, I didn't want a blindfold. He agreed. We then waited for the Japanese to come for us.

As the day brightened we saw no one except the guards and the sentries who had been with us throughout the night. The Japanese officer who had given the order to shoot us finely arrived and said he had received a radio message the previous night ordering us brought to Rangoon. Then he left.

The gospel writer John said in John 15:13, "Greater love has no man than this that he lay down his life for a friend." The Lord spared me the supreme price that had to be paid for our heritage and our freedom. But many other men and women did - and still do - pay the supreme price so others may live free. I always considered myself a regular soldier, and I hope my recollections of that night in Burma, when we expected the Japanese to kill us, will be of some comfort to the families of those precious men and women who have died fighting for freedom.

Chapter 6

Rangoon City Jail

A truck arrived with a driver and two guards to take us to Rangoon. They again tied our hands and feet. The Japanese soldier in charge told us we were going to the Rangoon Prison Camp where we would have good food, a bed and good treatment. He had a little silly grin as he gave us this information, though.

Meiktila was about 350 miles from Rangoon on the road to Mandalay "where the flying fishes play," as Kipling wrote. However, we didn't see any flying fishes along the rough cut country road. August is in the middle of Burma's monsoon season. The first day on the road the rain was light and we managed to stay relatively dry in the bed of the uncovered truck. The Japanese guard who rode with us had a rain coat but we only had the cloths we were wearing when shot down. The rainfall steadily increased all the way to Rangoon.

Leisure and I had had nothing to eat or drink since being shot down. We were tired and hungry. When we reached the small village named Taungoo, the Japanese took us to a room that had two small cots with mosquito netting over them. They were not exactly the finest accommodations, but it would be almost two years before I would again sleep on any type of bed. Leisure and I, having been awake for two days, fell asleep almost immediately. We enjoyed a fitful sleep until the Japanese roused us just after sunrise with some watery soup and a handful of rice.

As the truck approached Rangoon we were blindfolded. I did not understand this unless the Japanese simply did not want us to know our directions in the city. When the truck stopped and the blindfolds were removed we were in front of what I later found out was Judson College. This school was known as Rangoon University. The Japanese were using the school as their headquarters for the entire Burma Theater. It was here, at the Japanese headquarters, where I and other POWs returned to build a large air raid shelter.

A smartly-dressed Japanese officer and two soldiers appeared. We were ordered to sit in the back seat of staff car - a black 1940 Chevrolet. (When the Japanese captured Burma there were many American supplies on the docks that had been provided for British. This car was probably part of those captured supplies.) The officer got in the front seat with the driver and one of the soldiers got into the back with Leisure and I.

Judson College was on the outskirts of the city and the Rangoon City Jail was downtown. It was about a four mile drive to the jail. As we drove through the city we could see the rubble and the bombed out buildings. These were the remnants from the Japanese battle against the British to capture the port city. I said to Leisure, "Look at that mess. Why haven't they cleaned up anything?" Then to my shock and surprise the young Japanese soldier sitting with us said, in crisp English, "Were you men flying in the B-25 North American aircraft?" This so surprised me all I could say was, "Yes." Leisure and I remained silent during the rest of the trip to the prison.

The interrogator at the Rangoon City Jail later told me that this young man had been attending the University of Washington in 1941. He returned to Japan for the Christmas holiday then when the war started on December 7, he entered the army as an interpreter. I believe he asked the question in the staff car just to let us know that he could speak and understand English.

Aerial view of Rangoon Prison. Photo taken after liberation.

Rangoon Central Jail, as the prison camp was called, was located in the southwest section of Rangoon only two blocks from the harbor and docks. It was bound on the north by St. John's Road, on south by Commissioner Road, on the east by Pongyi Street and on the west by Keigh Lry Street. It had served as a British prison camp during the colony days but had been condemned by the British in 1938. When the city fell to the Japanese in 1942 they converted it to a prisoner of war camp, although it was not officially designated as such until the last year of the war.

The jail was enclosed within a circular exterior wall. Inside were various cell blocks. The compounds were arranged similar to spokes in a wheel. The first prisoners to arrive at Rangoon were Dutch, followed by the British in February 1942.

The first American prisoners of war arrived in Rangoon on June 4, 1942. They were part of a B-17 crew that had been with General Haynes' group before the war started and were originally scheduled to be part of Doolittle's Tokyo raid.

On June 4, 1942, Major Douglas Sharp was serving as pilot, Lieutenant Herbert Wonderlick was the co-pilot, the navigator was Jack Horner, George Wilson was the bombardier and the crew chief Sergeant Malok. Sergeant Radcliff was the radio operator. This lone B-17 flew a bombing mission over Rangoon and was attacked by 23 Japanese Zeros. In a brutal fight that lasted more than half an hour, the waist gunner was killed and the other gunner was wounded. However,

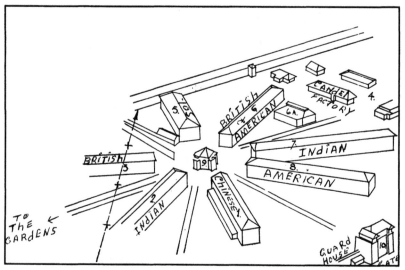

Sketch of Rangoon Prison Camp.

the crew did down four Zeros. Sharp and Wonderlick took the plane into a cloud bank where they lost the Zeros. But the bomber lost two engines and had a severed right tail rudder. The plane was on fire. Major Sharp ordered the crew to bail out.

When the B-17 emerged from the cloud bank the Zeros were gone and the smoke inside the plane had diminished. Sharp decided to keep going. As darkness fell, however, he and Wonderlick crash landed the plane in a rice field. The two pilots made their way to a British-controlled village then eventually back to India. The crew that had bailed out were captured and taken to the Rangoon Central Jail. Three of these men were killed when the Americans accidentally bombed the prison camp. Horner, Wilson and Radcliff were liberated with the other prisoners in May 1945.

First Lieutenant Koshima was commandant of the Rangoon Prison from June 1942 to April 1944. It was during this time that prison conditions were at their worst. Captain Motozo Tazumi was commandant for about one year, from April 1944 to April 1945 and Harvo Ito was chief officer of Rangoon Prison when the liberation began. Tazumoi was generally considered to be the most reasonable and considerate commandant at the camp.

Sergeant Major Wano San (san means "mister") was the quartermaster of the Rangoon Prison Camp. Brigadier General Ken Hichi Masuoka was the Japanese Kempeitai commandant at Rangoon in 1943 and part of 1944. The Kempeitai were the Japanese secret police, and they were brutal in their tactics. The secret police commandant from the later part of 1944 to April 1945 was Matad Jumei.

Inside the prison the wagon wheel cell blocks were surrounded by a wall so that each building had its own inner court. Each block was numbered. Block one was for the Chinese. Block two was for the Indians. Block three was for the British. Block four was for the Dutch (although the Dutch were only in Rangoon during the first part of 1942). Block five was solitary confinement. Block six held both British and Americans. Block seven was for Indians and block eight also held Americans.

Cell block five, the solitary confinement block, was a two-story block building that contained forty, 9 ft. by 12 ft. cells on each floor. Each had a 3 ft. by 6 ft. barred door and a single 4 ft. by 4 ft. barred window. The windows were high - you had to stand on your toes to see out - but if you looked through the window you could see the second floor of number six block. Each floor was divided by a 12 ft. hallway with twenty cells on each side of the hall. It was a secure building.

All the other cell blocks in the prison were two-story buildings containing four cells on each floor. Each cell was approximately 20 ft. by 55 ft. with a 15 ft. ceiling. Each cell had five 4 ft. by 8 ft. barred windows and another 4 ft. by 10 ft. barred window. There was also a corridor running the length of each floor between the cells and around the outside walls. Heavy wooden bars separated the cells and the perimeter corridor, which had five heavily-barred windows. Each compound had its own court yard.

In the solitary confinement block, as in all the other cell blocks, British ammunition boxes were used for toilets. These were carried out and emptied once a day. Each of the regular compound blocks had a frame building with open sides. They also held ammunition boxes that served as toilets. A hole in the ground served as a urinal. Each compound also had a cement trough about 30 ft. long, two ft. wide and three ft. deep. These were designed to carry water from the Rangoon city water system. But due to heavy bombing the system was frequently out of order. This trough supplied all the water for drinking, cooking and occasional bathing.

All water used for cooking or drinking had to be boiled. Each compound had its own cook house. These "houses" were basically open air shelters that covered a rice vat. Cooking pots and pans were made by the prisoners from scrap tin. They were kept in the cook house. Eating utensils were also made by the prisoners from scrap metal. Each prisoner had a single pan and a tin or bamboo drinking cup. Since we couldn't drink the water without boiling it first, tea leaves were boiled repeatedly. It made for very weak tea.

Each day individual compounds were given an allotment of raw rice. The Japanese provided a 1,200 calorie serving for each man on a work party and a 900 calorie serving for each sick man. The prisoners in each compound were responsible for their own cooking. The only other issue was a grass sack or threadbare blanket. The clothes you had were the ones you were wearing when shot down. Occasionally, some paper was smuggled in to roll cigarettes. We had no tobacco, so we used pipas leaves and cigarettes butts for smokes. Sometimes, we were able to purchase a Burmese cigar and crumbled that up for smokes.

The Japanese deposited Leisure and I at the Rangoon prison about 6 p.m. on August 5, 1943. It was raining; a warm, miserable, pouring rain. I was suffering from the burns on my face and hands and couldn't walk due to the injuries I suffered by bailing out near treetop level. With difficulty I could stand and shuffle my feet.

We entered the guard house and were lead into a small office. The room was empty except for a single wooden table and three chairs. Prison commandant Koshima was present along with two guards. Two other guards stood at the door behind Leisure and I. Another soldier was standing to our right with two dogs secured by a leash. A young interpreter was standing to the left of Leisure. The dogs were growling and straining at the leash. The soldier would let the animals lunge to within a few inches of my feet before pulling them back. This produced a general round of laughter from the Japanese. Because of the pain in my feet, legs and lower abdomen I was sitting with my legs stretched in front of me. The interpreter asked me to tuck in my legs. I did this and the Japanese restrained the dogs.

Koshima asked us for our name, rank and the type of aircraft that we had been flying. After a brief exchange he ordered us taken to solitary confinement.

I was forced to walk and my movements were slow, but the guard was patient. As we passed number six block I saw through the open courtyard a tall iron fence surrounding the building. I could see four or five people walking around in the courtyard. They bowed to the Japanese as they walked by. Leisure and I didn't understand this behavior. What amazed us, though, was the prisoners' appearance. They were each wearing only a loincloth, but they were walking skeletons. Absolutely skin and bones. This shocked me. I turned to Leisure and asked him if he thought we'd be looking like that soon.

His said yes. And he turned out to be right.

I later learned that these "skeletons" were British commandos and had been at the prison since 1942.

A concrete wall surrounded three sides of the solitary building. A tall iron fence and gate crossed both the front of the building and the courtyard. You entered the building by passing through this gate and the 12 ft. wide courtyard that extended from the gate to the building.

Just inside the building a stairway leading to the second floor, which had the same basic cell and hallway configuration as the ground floor. Facing the solitary building, the second-floor left corner cell held a British prisoner of war. From his second floor window this man could see the main gate of the solitary compound. He could also see above the compound's perimeter fence to number three block, which was under the command of British Brigadier General Clive Donald Hobson.

Leisure and I were placed together in a cell facing the foot of the stairway. When the Japanese left, the "clang" of the iron gate made a sickening sound. The cell was empty except for the latrine ammunition box and a 3 ft. by 6 ft. board sitting on four bricks. This was the bed.

They brought each of us a thin rag of a blanket. The Japanese also gave Leisure a small, hand-made mess tin. We had eaten a single bowl of watery soup during the previous two days but arrived at the jail too late for supper. Our next meal would be breakfast at the prison on August 6 - and the first meal since we left our squadron on August 3.

I asked the guard for a mess tin. He walked away but returned seconds later with a rough metal pan. I didn't realize it at the time, but this simple request would almost kill me. The guard was taken the mess tin from the cell of a prisoner who had died from dysentery. The next morning they removed his body. Within days I would be seriously ill with the disease.

As soon as the guards left we heard an Englishman's voice from the top of the stairway. It was like music to our ears, but his sound didn't match his story. There was no mistaking the English dialect. But the man said his name was Terry Melvin. He claimed to be an American lieutenant and a B-25 pilot who had been shot down near Prome. He asked us what we were flying. We told him a B-25 and that Leisure was the engineer and I was the radio operator.

I didn't know who this man was but I was sure he was not an Air Force lieutenant. I later told Leisure, "He doesn't sound like an American pilot to me."

He wasn't an Air Force pilot. But he was someone special.

*Top Right: Two prisoners eating a typical meal at Rangoon Prison. **Bottom Right:** A group of British prisoners from the medical section of Rangoon Prison after liberation.*

Chapter 7

Ras

Roy Anthony Stephen "Ras" Pagani was born July 23, 1915 at Fulham, England. His English father and French mother separated when the boy was four. At age 10 Ras went to an all boys Catholic convent. He stayed there until he was 13, when he was returned to his mother and began to look for work.

In July 1933, at the age of 18, he went for a bike ride one day and passed a army recruiting station. He went in and said that he wanted to join, but at five feet, five inches he was an inch shy of the required height. The recruiting sergeant said if he could stretch a little higher. Pagani raised his heels a bit and was instantly accepted.

He served a tour in India from 1934 to 1937 then returned to England. He was married in 1939 and was training in England when the war started with the Germans. In October 1939 he sailed for France. He spoke fluent French and was used as an interpreter. On May 10, 1940, the Germans invaded Holland and Belgium. For the next three weeks Pagani took part in the fighting withdrawal from Dunkirk. He reached Dover on June 1, 1940.

R.A.S. Pagani, age 30, on his release from captivity, 1945.

Pagani's unit sailed for Egypt in October 1941, but when the Japanese entered the war on December 7 this division was diverted to India then to Singapore. The winding journey left them at sea for nearly three months.

On February 5, 1942 as their ship *Empress of Asia* was 10 miles from the Singapore docks it was attacked by five Japanese bombers. One bomb found the ship's funnel and set the *Empress* a blaze. The men were forced to evacuate.

After reaching the docks they were re-equipped and placed with the 18th Army Division in Singapore. On February 15 their position came under heavy Japanese shelling. By mid-afternoon

Pagani was ordered to collect all of the division's arms. Orders had been cut: Singapore would surrender that evening.

Major D. R. Lullineux had assumed command of the 18th Division. Pagani reported to the major that he was unable to comply with the order to surrender and that he intended to attempt an escape. The major wished him luck. Pagani left at dusk for the Singapore docks.

Unable to crank the engines on any of the several motor launches tied at the docks, Pagani spotted about a 15-foot sampan. It was loaded with fish dung but had a rudder and a small sail, so he decided to take it.

As Singapore burned the sampan slowly moved across the calm water. Pagani slumped over the tiller and peered into the darkness, struggling to stay awake. He was exhausted and realized that if he were to keep the boat on course he would have to go ashore and get some rest. He landed and secured the little boat and promptly fell asleep.

He awoke the next afternoon and realized that if he were to have a chance of escape he would have to move from island to island, traveling at night. He adopted this plan and when darkness fell he set off again. Just before dawn he landed on another island and made contact with some friendly Malayans. They gave him some food and kept watch while he rested. In the evening he continued on his journey. Early the next morning he stopped at another island where he found a Chinese merchant who again fed him and allowed him to rest. Before dawn on February 19, four days after he had fled Singapore, he pulled into another island and found a party of British soldiers. They were part of an escape chain to Sumatra. Their job was to provide provisions for escapees. When they thought the last of the escapees had passed then they, too, would travel to Sumatra. The British soldiers advised Ras to go to Sumatra because the chances of surviving an open ocean voyage to Australia in such a small boat were slim. Ras took the advise and after some food and rest left that evening bound for Sumatra.

During the second night he was caught in a terrible storm. He lowered the sail and secured the boat. But as the storm intensified. Waves repeatedly broke against the side of the boat. Fearing he would be thrown into the sea, Ras lay flat across the boat and clung to the gunwales.

For hours he clung desperately to the little boat. He found strength in prayer but said in his own heart that he could find little hope for survival. But he certainly did pray.

Then just before dawn the gale stopped as suddenly as it had started. The sea was still rough but at first light he made out a dark line in the water. He untied the lashings and hoisted the sail. He found himself about a mile out from a stretch of low lying land. He sailed straight for the wide mouth of a river. After creeping up the river for several hours he finally saw a small group of men. They waved that he should come ashore.

They were British soldiers; another link in the escape change he had discovered on Moro. He had made it to Sumatra - and for the moment was safe from the Japanese.

Ras traveled to Padang a port city on the west coast of the island. He arrived there around March 1, 1943 and waited for a ship to arrive and take them to India. Several ships had already been loaded with as many men, women and children that could be packed into them and left. Everybody was eager to leave Sumatra before the Japanese arrived.

On March 15, Ras and the other escapees were told that Japanese troops were approaching Padang and that it would be wise to stay off the city streets after 10 p.m. Determined to escape, Ras joined some of the survivors from the *HMS Prince of Wales*. They spotted a small steam tug at the docks. It was hardly a suitable candidate for an ocean voyage but it was the only vessel available and the situation was becoming desperate.

The men loaded the boat, prepared it for sea, and on March 17 steamed across the harbor just a few hours ahead of the Japanese army. They didn't make it. A detachment of Indonesian soldiers fired a machine gun across their bow and ordered back to the docks.

The Japanese herded approximately 1,200 prisoners into a barracks. These prisoners included Australians and Dutch and about 500 British. The Japanese were unprepared for the task of taking care of POWs so they left them to look after themselves within the confines of the barracks. No rations were issued. Food was supplied by a Chinese contractor. The prisoners had to pay for their food. Otherwise they didn't eat.

The Japanese ordered the prisoners to form out in groups of 20 officers and 480 enlisted men. The men were then split into four companies and taken by rail to Fort Dekok, about 100 miles north of Padang. They passed Medan and arrived at the small port of Belawan Deli. From there they were loaded in the hold of a ship and sailed for the south Burmese coast.

The convoy arrived at Mergui on the May 25, 1942. This was the same day I left Charleston, South Carolina, with the 22nd Bomb Squadron on the *Mariposa* bound for India.

While in Mergui the POWs responded to work orders by doing as little as possible. On October 21 they were again herded into barges and shipped down river where two ships were waiting to take them to Moulmein. This was about the time the 22nd bomb squadron flew their first bombing raid to Hong Kong and Canton, China.

The POWs were marched into the railroad station at Moulmein. The next day they traveled by train about 30 miles to Thanbyuzayat, a railway station between Moulmein and Ye. This was also an intended junction for the railroad to Bangkok - a rail junction the POWs were to build. This became the infamous Japanese 18KM prison camp on the River Kwai

The brutal 18KM prison camp was under the command of a Japanese Colonel Nagitomo. The day after the prisoners arrived at 18 KM camp, Nagitomo made a speech that was a strange mixture of friendliness and threats. One thing, however, was perfectly understandable. That was his emphases on the total impossibility of a successful escape. He said if a man tried to escape he would see the jungles to the east and the ocean to the west and to the south. The Japanese army was positioned to the north.

The work was hard and the living conditions miserable. Huts leaked. Clothing and bedding was scarce. In October the pounding monsoon rains turned working conditions into a mud pit. Ras realized that to have the stamina for even a chance at a successful escape, he would have to go soon.

He formed two plans. One was to head to the sea, which was about 10 miles west of 18KM Camp. Once there he would steal a boat and move north along the Burmese coast to India. If unable to find a boat, he would double back to Moulmein and head north by land toward Burma. Neither plan was ideal but the second posed serious problems. It was about 600 air miles to the allied forces, but he would be facing a 1,000 mile journey on foot through hard country where he didn't speak the language. He would also be vulnerable to malaria and dysentery and other illness.

Ras had, however, prepared himself for this journey. He was now as brown as a native and his feet were hard for the trip (to pass as a native he would have to travel without shoes). He had a full brownish-red beard. He looked like a Burmese native, and the Japanese would be looking for an Englishman. Two days after he set his plans, Ras decided to leave the next morning.

At dawn he had breakfast, attended roll call, then joined the men who were reporting for sick call. The Japanese always attended the sick parade and any man that they judged able to work was beaten for wasting time, given a changkul, which was a hoe, and was told to join the working party immediately.

The Japanese were so confident that escape was impossible, they never sent a guard with a man who was going to join the working party. That morning, Ras took the beating then left the camp alone carrying is changkul. When he was about 100 yards from the camp gate he simply slipped off into the jungle.

Ras knew that he would not be missed until the evening roll call and guessed that the Japanese would not begin looking for him until the following morning.

He reached the Bay of Bengal in about four hours but failed to find a boat. Since he was only about 10 miles from the Japanese camp he didn't spend much time searching for one. He switched to his alternative plan. He would move northeast on foot until he reached the railroad, then turn north toward Moulmein.

When he reached the small village of Thanbyuzayat near Moulmein Ras was still only about 25 miles from the 18KM prison camp. Instead of waiting for darkness he put on his pagri (a turban worn by the Indians), rubbed dirt on his legs and face and walked down the main street.

This proved to be a risky maneuver. He caught the attention of several villagers, then saw a five-man guard of Japanese soldiers walking toward him. He overcame the natural instinct to run and instead casually walked toward a house to urinate. In India it was common for the men to simply squat in public to urinate. Since his survival depended on passing as a native Ras followed the local custom. He squatted with his back toward the Japanese and held his breath as they passed.

He entered a marketplace and found a stall with a curtain across the front. He slipped in, pulled the curtain and fell asleep.

He awoke after sundown. Ras left his hiding place and continued on his way until he reached the railroad which ran north toward Moulmein. He walked throughout the night, and as dawn approached he came to a small hut on the edge of a rice patty. He found an Indian family who nervously let him in and allowed him to sleep. He walked all the next night and by dawn was within a few miles of Moulmein. He left the railroad and found another hut.

An Indian emerged and they exchanged a few words. The man introduced himself as Muhammad Esoof and said that he had served several years in the Indian army. He was strongly pro-British. Esoof advised Ras not to enter Moulmein and not to attempt to swim across the Salween River.

Esoof told Ras that his brother was a fishermen who owned a good boat . This brother agreed to take Ras to the north bank of the Salween River and bypass the city of Moulmein. The journey took about an hour. When the boat rounded on the north shore Ras jumped ashore and waved good-bye to the helpful fisherman.

After a couple of days travel Ras noticed that the surrounding trees had the managed look of a plantation instead of the wild growth of a jungle. He left the railroad and moved through the trees until he came to some well-kept buildings. He watched the property and soon discovered that the people who lived in the houses were not Burmese. The place had an unmistakable feel of prosperity. He surmised that the people had prospered under the British and most likely did not look upon the Japanese with good favor. He decided to ask for help.

The door was opened by a surprised servant who motioned that Ras should wait. When the door re-opened Ras found himself standing before a well-dressed, attractive young woman. In clipped English she said, "Please come in."

Ras couldn't believe the surroundings. Lace curtains, Victorian furniture. Several small tables holding framed portraits. His hostess talked to Ras about her family. She said that they were Karen Christians and her father's name was Saw ("mister") Po Thin, who, along with his family, had been educated in England and had a high admiration for the British. She said her father was a timber merchant who had been contracting with the Japanese to produce timbers for the railroad they were building to Siam. The name of their hamlet was Kyawaing, and it was located only few miles from Thaton.

Ras told Saw Po Thin about his adventures; the escape from Singapore, surviving the storm at sea, his time as a POW and his escape from the 18KM camp. Ras also told the man of his intentions to reach allied forces in northern Burma and asked Saw Po Thin to help. The timber merchant told Ras that it would be nearly impossible for an Englishman to move west without being captured by the Japanese or detected by the Burmese.

Po Thin told Ras about a British major who lived the Karen hills and trained Karen gorillas to fight the Japanese. This man's headquarters was only a few days journey from their hamlet. He could have Ras taken there. What Po Thin didn't tell Ras was that he had already sent a runner to the major to inform him of the Englishman's arrival and seek his advice.

The British major ordered that this Englishman should be brought to his camp. Ras left early the next day, cleverly concealed in a garbage cart. After passing safely through a Japanese check point, Ras and his escort abandoned the wagon, continued on foot eventually coming to a dirt road where another cart and driver were waiting. Ras' escort introduced the new cart driver as Saw Willie Saw, who had worked as a civilian for the British.

Ras was now the Karen States, where he would be relatively safe from both the Japanese and the Burmese, both of whom feared the Karens as deadly guerrilla fighters. The two men soon reached the village of Molopa.

Two days later Saw Willie Saw informed Ras that they were going to visit the Catholic priest. They arrived at a village named Kodaingti where they found a mixed population of Karens, Indians and Gurkaks. The Gurkaks had been separated from their regiment during a fight at Sittang Bridge and had joined the Karens. Ras also met Lance Mura, a former Burmese rifle soldier. Mura took over as Ras' body guard and remained with him for the rest of his journey north.

Ras was eventually lead at a rough bamboo jungle shelter that was occupied by a Kachin, which were another ethnic group living in Burma. The Kachin lead the party through the jungle until they came to another jungle hut where they found a tall dark-skinned man dressed in native clothing.

Ras didn't recognize this man as a British officer. He thought he was another native until the tall, gangly major walked out to meet him and said, "Hello, old chap. How are you?" It was as though he were welcoming Ras to his English country home. This very English-type greeting caught Ras off guard.

All he could find to say was, "OK, sir."

It was a heartwarming moment. The man introduced himself as Major Hugh Seagrim. He grasped Ras' hand and in a voice choked with emotion kept telling him how glad that he was that he had come. After the trials and fears Ras had experienced during the past few months he felt his eyes fill with tears at this greeting.

Ras closely studied this Englishman who was to have such a profound influence on his life. Ras got the impression that Seagrim had instantly sized him up, and now they were already firm friends. Ras has stated that he will always believe God sent him to Hugh Seagrim.

Ras told Seagrim about his travels and his escape from the Japanese 18KM prison camp. He also knew the Japanese were probably looking for an escaped POW Pagani. Seagrim and Ras decided that he would be known as Corporal Ras. They thought this would be a name the Japanese would not associate with an escapee by the name of Pagani.

Ras spend 10 days with Seagrim, and the two men formed a close relationship. Ras regarded Seagrim as the most remarkable officer with whom he had ever served. He was willing to help the major in any way possible.

Seagrim told Ras about the Karens and the other hill tribes of eastern Burma. It was the Karens' widespread conversion to Christianity that most interested Seagrim. Some were Buddhist, but many had embraced Christianity in one form or another, mainly as Baptists or Roman Catholics, depending on local missionaries. These devoted missionaries, like Seagrim, were dedicated to the Karens and lived as they lived in the villages.

Ras told Seagrim that his objective was to travel north and join forces with the allies in northern Burma, eventually joining the British 14th Army. Seagrim tried to talk Ras out of his plan. He said it would be nearly impossible for one man to make the trip safely. But Ras was confident. He explained to Seagrim that with the help of some Karen guides, he thought that he could reach the coast where he could find a boat and head north.

They spent their final day together making preparations for Ras' journey. Early the next morning Ras said good-bye to Seagrim and started for Pyagawpu to collect a gun from the stockpile of weapons that Seagrim and the Karen guerrillas had cached. As he neared the jungle he looked back and saw Seagrim. He suddenly seemed like a very lonely figure and at that moment Ras almost regretted his enthusiasm for his journey. But then Seagrim raised his hand in a farewell salute. Ras returned the salute and continued on through the clearing. It was the last time he had the opportunity to speak to the British major.

Ras left accompanied by Lance Mura. Seagrim had also sent his personal guard of eight men to escort Pagani. When they reached Pyagawpu, Ras and Mura were taken to the house of a Baptist minister where they found a case of weapons.

While Ras was at Kadiangti he also became re-acquainted with Saw Po Thin, the timber merchant who had first directed him to Seagrim. Ras then learned that Saw Po Thin was a powerful force behind the Karen resistance movement. His work for the Japanese in supplying timbers for the Burma-Siam railroad enabled him to move freely about the forest in the Karen States. Po Thin kept Seagrim informed as to the Japanese intentions and troop movements. He also supplied the guerrillas money and arms. The Karens told Ras that this generous man also gave large sums of his own money so that young Karens could train in the medical field.

Ras and his party moved north toward Irrawaddy River. He sent the Karen guides back to their territory while he and Mura continued on toward the Irrawaddy and into the most dangerous part of their journey.

Ras calculated that it would take six days to reach the Arakan Yomas, the coastline area of Burma which was home to Karen villages. Along the way they would have to cross the Irrawaddy River.

The next day Mura was captured by some villagers. It was a fight from which Ras narrowly escaped.

He had another brush with capture while resting at a Buddhist temple. He continued his journey toward the Irrawaddy and after a couple of days, arrived at a Burmese pagoda. He was greeted by a monk who spoke broken English. Ras accepted the monk's invitation for some food and rest.

While napping he was awakened by the sound of aircraft and rushed outside. They were American B-25s bombing Prome, a city about 150 miles north of Rangoon. I was on some bombing missions over Prome and there's a good chance that I was in one of those bombers.

As Ras watched the American bombers he developed a new strategy about his identity. He knew that if the Japanese captured and recognized him as the escaped prisoner Pagani, he would be returned to 18KM camp and shot. He decided to become a lieutenant in the United State Air Force. He thought the Japanese would be less likely to link an American Air Force officer with a British noncommissioned officer. He also decided to take his son's Christian names. Ras had a baby boy named Terry Ashton Melvin Pagani. He decided to take the names Terry Ashton as his Christian names, and Melvin as his sir name. When Leisure and I first met Ras in solitary confinement in Rangoon he introduced himself as Lieutenant Melvin.

With one more night's walk, he reached the Irrawaddy River - his last hurdle. The Arakan Yomas, home of the friendly Karens, lay beyond the river. He said good-bye to the monk and reached the Irrawaddy the next morning.

When he reached the Irrawaddy, Ras searched for a boat but failed to find one. The river was about a half-mile across at this point but Ras was a powerful swimmer. Before starting across, however, he took a note Seagrim had written to army headquarters, which included Ras' field promotion to sergeant, and destroyed it, along with his identity card.

After the moon rose that evening, Ras waded into the river. He was intent on swimming to the opposite shore and to the relative safety of Karen territory. About 150 yards from the bank he was caught in a strong undertow that, coupled with the weight of his gun and ammunition, threatened to pull him under. He dumped his gun and spare ammunition and floated downstream, but the current pushed him back onto the east bank of the river.

A couple of Burmese men approached. They helped Ras into their fishing boat but before they could leave a mob of about 50 Burmese arrived. Ras could see that they were armed with a few shotguns and dahs. When they ordered the fishermen to remain on the bank Ras knew his struggle for freedom had ended. It was a bitter moment.

Ras was tied and lead away but still managed to make a brief escape, slipping his ropes and dashing toward the jungle. But he stumbled and fell and another dash was stopped by a gunshot wound in the side. The Burmese were on him in seconds.

Beaten and bloody, Ras thought of his wife and young son and his promise that he would return home. That promise would now be broken. They would never know what happened to him. He had destroyed his identity papers and was now going to die alone, in the darkness near a muddy river in a distant land among a hostile people.

The Burmese placed him face down in a boat and took him to a Japanese outpost where a doctor roughly stitched the worst of his wounds. What medical attention was given, was done so in haste and without an anesthetic. The Japanese asked him where he had come from, and he replied that he was an American army officer who had been shot down the previous night. An ambulance soon arrived and Ras was taken to a hospital in Prome.

He fell into the hands of a Japanese physician who seemed delighted to inflict as much pain of possible. After a while, though, this tough Englishman passed through a pain threshold.

That night in the Japanese hospital was one Ras would not forget. At one point the pain became so intense he put a blood-stained towel over his face intent on suffocating himself. But remembering the promise to is wife, he threw the towel in a corner and survived the night. He slowly began to recover. When he was strong enough to speak, he was interrogated by the Japanese but stuck to his story about being an American officer shot down during a night raid over Prome. He explained his native clothing by saying that his uniform had caught fire, and the natives had given him what he was wearing. This story seemed to satisfy the Japanese.

Ras remained in the Prome hospital for about six weeks. Early one morning he was taken to the railroad station by two Japanese soldiers who escorted him to Rangoon. Upon arrival in the city they took him to the New Law Courts Building and turned him over to the Kempeitai - the Japanese secret police. This was bad news, for Ras knew that few of their prisoners lived long enough to be released.

Kempeitai was a word no prisoner wanted to hear.

He was placed in an 10 ft. by 8 ft. foot cell with five other prisoners. The men were not allowed to speak and were permitted to move only to reach the latrine bucket.

The next morning the Japanese came for one of the prisoners whom they proceeded to beat and kick down the hallway to the interrogation room. Easily within earshot of the other prisoners, the man was tortured and questioned for about two hours. Ras and his fellow inmates could hear the yelling of the Japanese mixed with the screams from the prisoner. When the man was returned to his cell his face was blood streaked, swollen and bruised. His fingers and toes were grossly swollen. The other prisoners were not allowed to help the man, else they be given the same treatment.

Each day the Kempeitai came for another prisoner and after a few days they came for Ras. He crawled out through the trap door of the cell and was beaten as he went down the hall into the first of three interrogation rooms. The room contained two chairs on which sat two Japanese soldiers holding canes. Ras was made to kneel between them. One man would question him in rough English. After each answer Ras was struck with the canes. This continued for about half an hour. He was then dragged into the next room where the set-up was the same except that one of the two Japanese men was an officer. Ras was made to kneel between them. The officer drew his sword. Each time a question was asked he would beat Ras with the flat edge of the sword. He would then place an empty pistol to Ras' head and dry fire the gun. The Japanese officer would then draw the sword and swing it swiftly toward Ras' neck, checking his swing at the moment it touched the skin. Ras later learned that some men had been beheaded when the officer misjudged his swing.

The third room held the worst punishment. It was designed like an old style wash house with a plain concrete floor and a drain in one corner. He was made to lie on his back on the floor. His arms and legs were then secured to rings that were fixed into the concrete. He was positioned so that his head was beneath a slow dripping tap. Every few seconds it loosed a drop that struck him between the eyes. Prisoners were left here for about a half of an hour then the Japanese would return with more questions. Sometime slivers of bamboo would be placed under the fingernails and toenails, inserted in his nostrils and in the genitals and set on fire. Ras assumed each prisoner questioned by the Kempeitai was subjected to similar punishment.

One morning they came for him, and he expected to endure another round of questioning and torture. But to his surprise he was put on a truck and delivered to the Rangoon City Jail and placed in solitary confinement on the second floor of number five block.

But for now, though, Ras Pagani knew he was a lucky man. He had survived the Kempeitai. It was a feat few men could claim.

Chapter 8

Seagrim and the Karens

Hugh Paul Seagrim was the youngest of five sons of Reverend Charles Seagrim and his wife, Mabel. Charles Seagrim was the clergyman of Whissonsett and Horningtoft, which were two small adjoining villages located near the center of Norfolk, England.

Reverend Seagrim, a witty and talented man, was happy to see his sons grow up in this pleasant, safe and happy English countryside environment. The Rector was the hub of these two communities and the boys took part in all the sports. Hugh Seagrim's religious background and his easy association with the local people in and around Norfork did much to prepare the war years and his work among the Karen Christians who lived in the hills of southeast Burma.

Major Seagrim's strong religious foundation insured his respect of the Karens and give him the courage and comfort required for the dangerous and primitive life he was to have with them in the jungle. It also enabled him to love the Karens in the same way he had loved the villagers in England. He received their love and loyalty in return.

The Karens called the Japanese "short legs" and the English "long legs." Major Seagrim was exceptionally tall by their standards and they affectionately referred to him as "granddaddy long legs."

Seagrim had intended to enlist in the royal navy but was rejected due to partial color blindness. He then followed the trail of his four brothers and joined the army. Seagrim was selected for the Indian army and spent one year in India.

He was then assigned to the Burmese Rifle Battalion. Seagrim loved to travel and while in India used his free time to visit the Himalayas and other places. He even visited Japan where he began to admire the people who would later become his enemy.

Major H.P. Seagrim.

When Seagrim returned to Burma he continued his travels, usually taking some Karens with him. They would often travel to some of the small mountain villages in the Karen State. Seagrim grew to love the Karens and remained with them after the Japanese invaded Burma.

Seagrim recognized the Karens potential as guerrilla fighters and thought it would be wise to subject them to conventional military training. His British commanders ignored this suggestion.

Seagrim also respected the Karens for their strong religious convictions. He set great store by the teaching and the language of the Bible and was never himself without a Bible during his travels or during his life with the Karens. This cemented his position among the Karens as a man of integrity and a leader whom they could respect.

In December 1941, only a few days after the Japanese attack on Pearl Harbor, the British army began recruiting members of Burma's Levi tribe, which - like the Karens - were a Burmese tribe that did not side with the Japanese. The Levis lived in the hills of Burma and were placed under the command of H.N.C. Stephenson, an officer in the Burma Frontier Service. Stephenson knew of Seagrim's work with the Karens. In January 1942 he asked that Seagrim be assigned to the Karen territory for organizing and training the Karen tribes for guerrilla warfare against the Japanese.

Seagrim welcomed the appointment. He was also determined that if the Japanese overran Burma he would stay behind to live and work with the Karens.

Seagrim went to Papun and began recruiting Karens. Abandoning formal training methods he concentrated on perfecting ambush and guerrilla warfare techniques.

Seagrim moved his headquarters to Pyagawpu, which is in the Karen hills of southeast Burma. In March 1942 General Stillwell and the British Burma Rifle Battalion passed through Pyagawpu on the retreat north toward China and India. This left Seagrim as the only British or American officer in the Karen states.

In March 1942 a 150-man force of the pro-Japanese Burmese Independent Army (BIA) arrived. Under the direction of the Japanese army the BIA announced it was taking over all administrative duties for the city - and that all arms would be handed over to it.

Soon after the BIA arrived their leader was ambushed and killed by the Levis. The BIA second in command, a rough cut character named Bohtunhla, took this as a reason to massacre 17 Karen elders who had been detained in prison in Pyagawpu.

The Levis attacked Pyagawpu and managed to rescue some Karens who were being held by the BIA. The Burmese Independent Army retaliated by arresting all the Karens they could find. Several Karen women were also attacked and the Karen villages surrounding Pyagawpu were burned. The BIA then moved to Bilin taking with them several Karen hostages. This act so outraged the Karens that they burned Pyagawpu to deny the BIA shelter if they returned. A state of war then existed between the Karens and the BIA and by the end of May 1942 the Levis and the Karens had driven the Burmese Independent Army out of Burma's Salween district. For the following five months Seagrim and his Karen guerrilla force continued to attack the BIA and the Japanese army.

By October 1942 the British major had organized a reliable intelligence network. He was providing allied army headquarters accurate information on bombing targets. Relying on information from this same Karen intelligence chain, Seagrim recommended that the New Law Courts Building in Rangoon not be bombed because many Karens were being held there by the Japanese army secret police.

By March 1943 Seagrim's Karen guerrilla army was continuing to harasses the Japanese, but several of his key people had been captured. The Japanese had also been searching for Seagrim. By January 1944 this search was taken over by the Kempeitai, who proceeded to terrorize the Karen villages.

Seagrim moved frequently to avoid capture. Many of the Karens who had worked with Seagrim told the Japanese that they believed the major had died in the jungle. It was a good story but one that didn't wash thoroughly with the Japanese. They would believe Seagrim was dead when they saw a body.

This prompted a grisly suggestion from one of the Indians who had parachuted into Burma to join Seagrim's band. His idea might have work had it been followed. He suggested that British army headquarters deliver by parachute a tall English corpse which the Karens would present to the Japanese as Seagrim. This plan was never executed.

The Kempeitai stepped up their pressure. They arrived at the village of Mewado and threatened to arrest and imprison all the Karens there unless Seagrim surrendered.

When the major learned of this he decided to surrender to save the innocent Karens additional suffering. In March 1944 he walked out of the jungle and surrendered to Inoue, the Kempeitai commander who had arrived in Mewado. Ba Gyaw, who had parachuted into Burma to join Seagrim, insisted on surrendering with him. He died in the Rangoon prison camp.

Seagrim was taken to the Rangoon Law Court Building which by this time also held several American fliers. Several of these airmen were later transported to the Rangoon prison camp where they freely testified that Seagrim was an inspiration to all who knew him.

There is no evidence that Seagrim was ever tortured by the Kempeitai. It seems that the Japanese, even the Kempeitai, respected his courage and were hopeful that he would use his influence with the Karens to cooperate with the Japanese. He steadfastly refused.

One of the Americans who was in the Law Courts Building with Seagrim had this to say about him:

> He never seemed to be sick. He was a very religious man who carried the Bible with him at all times. He would not call the Japanese master. He would not bow to them. He walked tall and straight with his head in the air. Always calm and friendly and doing what he could for his fellow men. He loved the Karen people as he loved his own and was dedicated to their freedom.

Seagrim was later moved to the Rangoon City Jail and housed in an isolated cell across from the guard house. On September 2, 1944, Ras Pagani was on a work party moving supplies near the guard house and main gate. He happened to look up and saw a Japanese truck leaving the jail. In the back of the truck with the guards was a tall Englishman and seven Karens. As they started through the breezeway toward the front gate the Englishman saw Pagani, gave him a big smile and waved to him. Pagani returned the wave as the truck pulled out of the prison. It was a few moments before Pagani realized that the Englishman was his beloved Major Hugh Seagrim.

That same day Seagrim was court-martialed and sentenced to death. He and the seven Karens were taken to Kemmendine Cemetery in Rangoon and shot. Seagrim pleaded with the Japanese to spare the Karens, repeatedly telling them that he was fully responsible for their guerrilla activities, and so only he should be killed. The Japanese ignored the pleadings and killed the eight men.

Seagrim's execution was another example of the treachery, deceit and hypocrisy so often shown by the Japanese military in Rangoon. The major had surrendered voluntarily to save the Karen people from further ill treatment. He was assured that he would be treated as a prisoner of war and that the persecution of the Karens would stop after he surrendered. However, the Japanese continued to terrorize the Karens until all resistance was crushed.

Actions like this stained the honor of the armed forces of Japan. They would pay a terrible price for their broken promises in Burma. In 1945 the Karens, newly armed by the advancing allies, fell upon the Japanese retreating forces and killed them without mercy.

Chapter 9

Solitary

John Leisure and I remained in solitary confinement 84 days. During this period Ras Pagani was a great help to us. He said that we could not stick to name, rank and serial number. "They can make you talk, and they will make you talk," he said.

Ras told us to make up a story and stick to it. "Keep it simple and easy to remember. If you do this then the Japanese will believe you are cooperating. Then when you tell them you don't know something they will tend to believe you."

Leisure and I followed this advice. We weren't going to reveal the location of our air base so when they asked me "What base were you stationed at?" I answered that we didn't have a base. We moved around from base to base. They then said: "You were in a B-25. Did B-25s raid Tokyo?" We'd answer yes. There was no reason to deny that.

When they asked, "Could they do this again?" The answer was yes, because the purpose of the raid was to let them know the city could be bombed anytime the Americans wanted to hit it. With this knowledge they would keep fighters in Japan guard Tokyo instead of sending them to the front.

The next question might be, "Where are the blind spots on the B-25?" The answer was that there were no blind spots - there's a top turret and belly guns, side guns, a tail gunner and a nose gunner. There were actually several blind spots, but they didn't know that and accepted our answer.

The next question was, "Are you a radio operator?" I'd tell them, yes, I was a radio operator.

"Can you send code?" The answer was no.

"Can you repair radios?" The answer again was no.

They'd say, "But you're a technical sergeant. Why can't you send code? Why can't you repair radios? What can you do?" I'd say that I call the control tower for landing instructions, and I operate guns. That's all.

Question: "You're a technical sergeant and that's all you do?" I'd answer, that's all. They just give us rank in the American Air Force.

Question: "How long have you been in India?" I'd answer that I'd just arrived. That way I couldn't know much about the theater. Actually, I had been in India more than a year.

The Japanese could force a man to talk. Ras had the right idea: put together a story and stick to it. (After World War II the Air Force began training their crews on what to say and not stick to name, rank and serial number. This alternative training to "name, rank and serial number" is taught today.)

Chinese prisoners delivered food to the cell blocks. The food consisted almost solely of rice, although we would sometimes have some stock brand (the type commonly fed to livestock) boiled in water. No salt, except on rare occasions, and very weak tea. The Chinese would pass down the hall distributing the food first then the tea. Occasionally as they made their final trip down the hall they would have some tea remaining. We would ask them for it and occasionally the Japanese guard would say yes.

Suffering from burns I craved water and wanted the tea more than food. I was hungry and thirsty the 84 days that I was in solitary and with the exception of a few days, I was hungry the entire time I was in the prison camp. I was not alone in my want for food. The other men were hungry and thirsty, too.

After the Chinese left with the food, a Japanese guard would have us empty the latrine ammunition box. Ras had told us that we were to bow each time a Japanese soldier passed by. One particular guard walked with a limp and he did not like Americans. We called him "limpy." He was called "Tarzan" by some of the other prisoners, though this had no reference to his size or strength.

If we failed to bow properly this guard would motion for us to come to the door of the cell. When we did he would then hit us on the head with his walking stick. It seemed to be a habit, because he did this almost every day to all the prisoners, and seemed to take great delight in doing so. We were told to bow again and, again, were struck on the head. We soon learned not to come to the cell door.

In April 1945 when the Japanese tried to evacuate some of us they gave us some old Japanese uniforms. This was the only time we received any clothing.

The Japanese took our flight jackets and all of our personal items. The clothing that we were wearing when captured was all that we had while in the prison camp. The mildew and dampness from the six month monsoon season quickly deteriorated our shoes and socks. We cut off our shirt sleeves and pants legs to use for towels, loincloths and bandages.

I was wearing my flight coveralls over my uniform so I had some extra clothing to use. We would wear our clothes, such as they were, for the daily roll call and when on work parties outside the prison.

Otherwise we generally wore a loincloth. We sometimes would even wear the loincloth after we got to the job site.

When a man died, his clothes, mess tin and other possessions where passed on to his "mucker," which is an English expression for a man's friend. Americans would call this the "buddy system." This is how I acquired a hat.

After a couple of days in solitary, Leisure and I began to rationalize our situation. We thought back to August 3 and wondered why McCook hadn't pulled up to about 2,000 feet and have everyone bail out, but then realized that we couldn't have stayed in the aircraft any longer than we did. I was badly burned when I jumped, and I was only in the plane less than a minute. We figured that McCook, not knowing our condition and not able to communicate, decided not to bail out and leave us in the tail. He instead tried to belly land the aircraft.

Our second day in solitary, we learned from Ras that the burial party had removed two men from the number six block and one man from number three block. From his cell on the second floor Ras could see several different cell blocks. We had seen the walking skeletons when we first came into the prison and now we were beginning to wonder if anyone would get out of this jail. We knew we were trapped until the allies re-took Burma. The question became, "Can we stay alive until liberation?"

Leisure and I shook hands and promised that if either one of us got out and the other did not, the survivor would visit the other man's family. John was from Compton, California. John died in the prison and, as promised, I did visit his home. But I didn't go until 1950 and it was too late. His father had died and his mother had re-married and moved to northern California. I have always regretted that I did not attempt to visit Leisure's family sooner. However, I did write to John's family and to those of my other crew members when I returned home.

My burned hands were still wrapped, and I was wondering how long I should wait before attempting to remove the bandages. I knew they were likely to stick to the flesh. Help arrived soon, however. When the Japanese opened the cell door later that day in walked an Indian dressed in a British officers uniform and wearing a big smile. I later learned that this was Captain B. N. Sudan. Captain Sudan was with the British Burma Medical Corps and had been captured when Burma fell to the Japanese.

The Japanese used Captain Sudan to treat their personnel at the camp. Sudan had seen Leisure and I when they brought us in, and I appeared to be in such bad shape that he pleaded with the Japanese to examine me.

He got right to work. "I'm Dr. Sudan," he said while listening to my chest through his stethoscope. He leaned forward and whispered into my ear, "Don't let these heathens get you down. Everything will be all right. God will see to that." I cannot describe the encouragement that brought.

He then said that all Americans have a strong heartbeat and changed the bandage on my left hand. As he left, Captain Sudan whispered that he would try to get back to see me.

From our window we could see the second floor of number six block where both British and Americans were being held. We could see two men standing in front of the second floor window but not so that they could easily be seen. They were waving their arms and making letters with their hands. The messages were, "I am Lieutenant Humphreys, P-38 pilot," and "I am Lieutenant Cotton, B-24 pilot." They asked for our names and if we were injured. They signaled that they would try to send up extra food through the Chinese. They occasionally did manage to do this.

An Indian in solitary had learned to pick the lock on his cell door. One night after the Japanese had left the building for the day, we saw him pass by our door. He was stooped very low and was on his way upstairs to see Pagani. He had a big smile on his face and waved to us as he went by our door. That was the first smile I'd seen in quite a while, and it was so welcome I can still see it today. We later learned that this was Lance Mura, the Indian who had been Ras' bodyguard when they were in the jungle with Major Seagrim. That night Mura told Ras that the Japanese were going to release him the next day. We never saw Mura again, nor did we ever learn what happened to him.

The Japanese interrogated us daily, always asking the same or similar questions. Each day Leisure and I would share what we had told the Japanese to help keep our stories straight.

I was still wearing my Mayfield High School class ring on my left hand, which was the most badly burned. The hand was beginning to swell around the ring and Leisure and I knew if we didn't get it off soon it was going to cause a serious problem. I asked the interrogator if he could get this ring cut off for me. The interrogator's name was Matsuda who we regarded as rather simple minded. However, he apparently had access to high places in the Japanese armed forces. This same man can be seen in the photograph of the Japanese surrender to General MacArthur and the allied commanders on the *USS Missouri.*

He is in the group standing at attention while waiting to sign the formal surrender. The next to the last Japanese officer in the second row is Matsuda. So he must have been much more important than we thought he was.

The next day Matsuda had Leisure and I brought into the room for interrogation. He brought with him a small rusty four-inch file. My hand was now badly swollen; the flesh peeling. Leisure used the rusty file to cut the ring.

Things got worse. After 12 days I developed dysentery. It was a helpless feeling to know that you were sick and that there was nothing that could be done for you. We passed this information to the Americans on the second floor of number six block. Lieutenant Cotton told Captain Sudan that I had dysentery. He persuaded the Japanese to let him see me, although there wasn't anything he could do other than provide moral support.

When the Japanese guards brought Captain Sudan into my cell he checked my heart again and asked me a few questions. The Japanese watched closely and allowed us to talk only about my condition. Captain Sudan gave me some powdered charcoal and a piece of paper and told me to take it at meal time. I was also told to count my number of

The Japanese surrendering on board the USS Missouri. Matsuda, my interrogator, is third from left on back row.

bowel movements as a way of keeping track of my condition. During the next few days my condition worsened. One night during about an eight hour period I passed blood and mucus 37 times. I grew extremely weak. At the time I did not realize the seriousness of my condition. Only after I began to improve did I realize how low I had been.

The frequency of the daily movements decreased. When I was released from solitary I was passing bowel dysentery only four or five times each day. This continued for about six months.

Toward the end of August, Burma was still in the grip of the monsoon season but that didn't stop the American bombing raids. The B-24s continued to pound the docks. These raids terrified the Japanese. The planes would come over in several flights of "V" and "box" formations, all dropping their loads at the same time. This approach was called "pattern bombing" and rained hundreds of 500 pound bombs at virtually the same time.

Occasionally, one of the planes would drop a few seconds late and cause the bombs to hit away from the target. They hit the prison camp three times killing several prisoners and guards. You never forget the sound of the bombs as they are falling. If you've ever stood on a railroad track and heard the rumbling of a train you know it grows louder as the train approaches. Then there's a tremendous roar as it passes. This is how the bombs sounded. When the bombs are falling around you, or hitting very close, you detect the thundering roar of a passing train.

During the early part of the war the jail was used as a visual location point for the bombing runs. The Americans would bomb during the day, appearing over the target around noon. After the monsoon season ended the British would bomb during the night. The Americans continued their daytime runs. We learned to tell the different planes by the sound of the engines, whether they were American, English or Japanese.

The Japanese were terrified of the bombing raids and the third time the allies hit the prison camp with stray bombs they grew worried. The Japanese ordered Lieutenant Cotton to go on the radio and tell the Americans that POWs were housed in the prison. Cotton's broadcast apparently made an impact because the bombing formations then started going around the prison camp.

Leisure and I passed the time communicating with Cotton and Humphreys. We did this simply by making letters in the air with our hands. I remember the old saying about living on bread and water. Leisure and I both would have given just about anything for a loaf of bread and some water. This would have really been a feast. It was then that I remembered the mutton that we had complained about on the *Mariposa*. John and I agreed that we would never again complain about food.

We kept track of our time in solitary confinement by making a daily mark on the wall. We also talked about our home life and learned about each others family and friends. We discussed how long it would take the allies to reach Rangoon and who would get there first, the Americans or the English. From where and when would the invasion come? What would the Japanese do? And what would they do with us?

I was still having trouble walking and was ill with dysentery. But that didn't stop a dose of regular abuse from the guards. Near the end of August the Japanese brought in Sergeant Andy Cowans, a Scottish fighter pilot who had broken his jaw while attempting a crash landing. The Japanese offered no medical attention. His jaw did eventually heal, but it was disjointed and affected his speech.

When you're locked up in a cell with a man for a long time, like Leisure and I were, you get to know a great deal about each other. We talked about our families and friends and what we would do when we got out of Rangoon and returned home. But we seldom discussed the possibility of dying in the prison although we both knew this could easily happen. As the months passed we saw our friends and comrades dying around us. The central question became: How long can we stay alive? We were sure the allies would win the war, but we had no way of knowing how long it would take.

The Japanese brought in a Dutch colonel and a Dutch captain and placed them in solitary. Sergeant Andy Cowans was in the cell next to us and the Dutch officers were placed in the cell next to Cowans. They had plenty of cigarettes and cigars and would pass these things to us occasionally. They seemed friendly and began questioning Sergeant Cowans about what he was flying and where he was flying from. We grew suspicious and when the Japanese took the colonel and captain out for interrogation Ras told us to be careful because they seemed suspicious to him, too. A few days later they were taken out of solitary and we never saw them again. I've always thought that they were Japanese informants trying to get information from us.

Leisure and I had been in solitary several weeks before we began to fully trust Ras. He had told us part of his story but it seemed so fantastic that it was difficult to believe. I was almost certain he was not an American, as he claimed to be. Leisure eventually accepted Ras' story before I did.

After a couple of months in solitary a group of Japanese Imperial Marine Officers paid us a visit. The guard and camp commander brought Leisure and I out for them to see. We must have appeared to be a sad lot after two months in solitary. We had lost weight and had been wearing the same clothes every day. The Japanese laughed and ridiculed us and took our pictures before putting us back in our cell.

Around this time a British soldier attempted an escape. He got through the main gates and wandered through the streets of Rangoon for about 24 hours before being re-captured. He was beaten and taken to number six block, shown to the others prisoners, then taken away. We assumed the Japanese shot the man. We never saw him again.

In late September 1943, the American bombers hit the prison for the first time since Leisure and I arrived. We heard the sirens at the same time that we heard the bombers overhead. When the bombs hit the ground the prison walls shook. One of the planes must have dropped their load late because each time a bomb hit it was closer to us. It sounded and felt though the bombs were "walking" toward the prison. I looked up at Leisure and said, "Do you think they're going to stop?"

He said, "I don't know." Just then they did stop. But the bombs had hit the Indian block and the number three block, which was next to solitary confinement. They killed several Indians and British soldiers along with three Americans who had been members of Major Doug Sharp's B-17 crew.

By the end of October 1943 several more prisoners had been moved into solitary, but they would not be in our company. Leisure and I were taken out of solitary confinement on October 28, 1943.

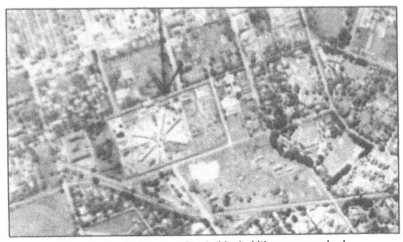

From the air, the Rangoon City Jail looked like a wagon wheel.

Chapter 10

Six Block

We were moved to number six block. My health was improving but the short walk from solitary to six block let me know that I was still weak.

Six block held about 120 prisoners. All were British POWs except for six Americans: Lieutenant Cotton, Lieutenant Humphreys, Lieutenant Moxley, Lieutenant Garrott, Sergeant Hickenbothem and Sergeant Crostic. When we were liberated in 1945, we still had between 110 and 120 men in six block, although prisoners had arrived regularly throughout 1944 and the first three months of 1945. The high death rate kept the block population from rising. The men died as quickly as new prisoners arrived.

Leisure and I were again amazed at the malnutrition and overall condition of the men. Many were mere skeletons. Men with beri-beri suffered from swollen legs and stomachs. We were both glad to be out of solitary and in a compound with other people.

I became friends with Lieutenant Walter Cotton. The B-24 pilot was a tremendous help to Leisure and I along with the other American enlisted men. When other American officers were brought to the prison camp Cotton was our communication link with the other officers.

Cotton also briefed Leisure and I on the conditions of the camp, including what we needed to do and what to expect. The ranking officer in six block was an English flight officer, which is equivalent to an American captain. We had the morning and evening roll call, which the Japanese called "tenko." Prisoners were required to be in formation when the Japanese arrived at the gate to the compound. Tenko was also conducted in the Japanese language. A separate formation was held for officers and enlisted men. The British flight officer would make the officers' report. Sergeant James Masterson would report for the enlisted men.

Tenko worked like this: each group, officers and enlisted men, would call their formation to attention. All commands were given in Japanese, and they had to be sharp and snappy. The next command was "eyes right." The men would then salute the Japanese. Then it was "eyes front." Then officer in charge would say "count off" and the men in the front line would count off: one, two, three . . . Again, everything had to be spoken in Japanese and had to be crisp and snappy. The men would stand in two lines. If possible we would line up with the same number of men in each line. This way the officer in charge could simply double the count. The reporting officer would then report to the Japanese.

The salute, the report and the count off had to be sharp and fast with no errors. Otherwise you were beaten.

The men would line up before the Japanese arrived and count off slowly. Each man would then know his number. This way when the Japanese arrived the count would go quickly.

The men were screened daily for work details. Men unable to work were placed in what we called the "hospital." This was actually just a separate building next to the main compound block building. It was divided into two sections: one large room where the daily patients were kept, and a smaller back room which we called the intensive care area. This is where the most severely ill patients were housed. No one wanted to go to intensive care. Few men emerged alive.

The hospital building had a solid roof and wooden slat walls with about a two inch crack between the boards. The floor was dirt. A walkway split the center of the room. On each side were wooden platforms about two feet high. These served as the patient beds.

The hospital had the smell of death - the smell of decaying flesh

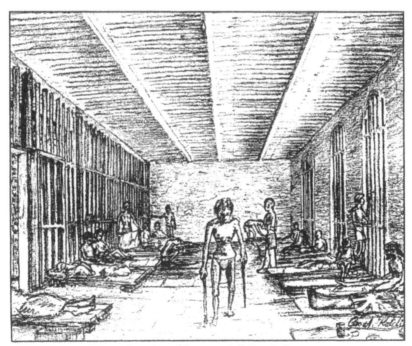

Drawing of Rangoon Jail Hospital.

and the stench of open dysentery toilets. Most of the men also suffered from jungle sores and scabies.

We did not have a doctor in six block at this time so Lieutenant Cotton acted as the medical officer. He would hold sick call each morning to screen the men for that day's work parties. "Healthy" prisoners were dispatched to do the hard manual work: unloading ships and boxcars, dig trenches, building air raid shelters, and other things. The "slightly sick" men were placed on a garden work detail inside the prison.

Lieutenant Cotton told me that I needed to be on my feet. Otherwise I would not survive. I had not yet recovered to where I could do demanding physical work so Cotton assigned me as his assistant to help him hold sick call. Cotton could do nothing for sick men other than listen to their problems. But this he did and it provided a huge psychological boost. Everyone understood that their mental attitude was a key ingredient in the struggle to survive.

Each morning the sick men would line up for sick call. Cotton would call each man by name and ask about their condition. Almost every man had the same answer: "Not too bad, sir." Cotton had been seeing these men for so long that he would often whisper to me, "This one has three weeks," or "This one has six weeks," and so forth. I never heard a single man complain. They just gradually faded away and died silently. Their courage in the face of hopelessness was remarkable. I still remember each man answering, "Not to bad, sir," as they reported to Cotton.

Men reporting for sick call were asked about the number of bowel movements they had experienced the previous night. Cotton's options for treatment were severely limited. But depending on the number of movements reported, Cotton would tell the man to take only tea for a few days to rest his bowel, or, eat only soft rice (which was prepared for some of the sick). He would sometimes gave the men some powdered charcoal and tell him to take it with some tea. The Indians insisted that powdered charcoal served a real medical purpose.

For the Americans the first few months in the prison were the worst. Strange as it may sound after a few months your body began to adapt to filthy, disease-ridden surroundings.

I had been in six block about a month when Cotton assigned me to the "garden party," which was made up of "slightly sick" enlisted POWs. The men, barefoot and usually dressed only in a loincloth and a hat (if a man was lucky enough to have a hat), would carry the ammunition box latrines to the Japanese garden and use the waste to fertilize the vegetables. The vegetable gardens were planted just inside the main outside wall. The latrine boxes would be emptied into two 40-gallon drums. These were then carried to the vegetable gardens. We would tilt the barrels and carefully pour out the waste from the dysentery-filled prison camp to fertilize the garden. We tried not go get the filthy stuff on us. But it was impossible to avoid splashes on our hands, arms, legs and feet.

While on the garden work party I wore my sleeveless khaki shirt for protection from the tropical sun. While working in the garden I often recalled what we were told upon arrival in India: "Don't get out in the sun even with a hat and proper clothing." In the extreme heat, we were warned, we would suffer sunstroke. This was obviously incorrect because if that had been true every member of the garden party detail would have been dead after the first day.

My hands had not completely healed from burns suffered when our plane was shot down. I could only partly open them and had difficulty handling a hoe to work for the garden work. After a several weeks I was kept in the compound for light duty.

I considered myself fortunate. All around me were men in worse condition.

Chapter 11

Goad

Lieutenant Harold Goad and his crew had been shot down in October 1943. Goad was the pilot of a B-24 from the 493rd squadron, 7th Bomb Group out of India. Their target had been the Rangoon Boat Works but the plane was shot down about 30 miles west of the city. Five members of the 10-man crew survived.

Eyewitness saw some of the men bail out, but Goad, with his parachute strapped on and his plane on fire, pulled out of the formation to protect the other aircraft. When last seen Goad was still in the pilot's seat. Smoke was pouring from the bomb bay compartment. The other planes in the formation watched as the wings collapsed on Goad's plane. The fuselage then broke in half and the aircraft disintegrated.

Goad had been flying at about 20,000 feet. Lieutenant Daniel Grinnan, co-pilot of the lead aircraft, reported that Goad's plane exploded with him aboard. This was true. But the pilot was blown from the aircraft and knocked unconscious. Goad fell almost 18,000 feet before regaining consciousness and opening his parachute. By then he was far to low to be spotted by any of the planes from his formation.

Goad was captured and brought to Rangoon Jail. But he had been declared dead because of Grinnan's report that he had seen plane explode with Goad still on board. When other men from his bomb group came into the prison they told Goad that he had been declared dead.

This worried Goad, a good-tempered man who was well liked by both enlisted men and officers throughout the prison camp. He told me and several other men that he had made his wife promise if he were killed, she would re-marry.

After Rangoon was liberated Goad learned that his wife had in fact re-married a few months before the war ended. When she learned of Goad's survival the wife had two options: she could divorce her new husband and return to Goad, or she could divorce Goad and re-marry her current spouse. She had her new marriage annulled and returned to Lieutenant Goad. They had twin sons and Goad became a commercial airline pilot. He died around 1960.

Chapter 12

Sudan, MacKenzie and Chi

Until November 1943 only 14 American airmen were in the Rangoon Prison Camp. But the 10th Air Force in India started a blitz on Rangoon during the last two months of 1943. By late November the number of American POWs began to increase. Several American airmen were brought to six block. These men included the remainder of Lieutenant's Goad's crew, Major Ramsey, Lieutenant Kellum's crew and others released from solitary confinement. This is when I met Perry Marshall, Don Davis, Bill Thomas and Charles Perry, each of whom were to become very good friends of mine.

Sergeant Perry Marshall was the engineer on Lieutenant Kellum's B-24 crew. He was from Obion, Tennessee, which is only about 50 miles from my hometown of Mayfield, Kentucky. We knew some of the same people. Meeting Marshall was almost like seeing someone from home.

As the number of Americans in six block increased the Japanese told us that we would have to separate the Americans and the British for roll call. Lieutenant Cotton told me that as the ranking noncommissioned officer I would have to hold tenko for the American enlisted men. Lieutenant Colonel Gilbert, who had just come into six block, would hold tenko for the American officers. A British officer and a British NCO would report for the British. We would now hold four different tenko formations.

I was still was very weak and had lost much weight but Cotton insisted I stay active. It was a key to survival. To prepare for tenko Cotton taught me to speak and count in Japanese. I don't know how I got through my first tenko without being beaten. But I did.

By this time Ras Pagani had been released from solitary confinement and had been moved to number six block. He was still passing himself off as an American officer and was kept with the American officers.

Lieutenant Colonel Douglas Gilbert and Major Gene Lutz along with several other officers and enlisted men were now in our block. Gilbert was the commander of the Americans in six block. Major Leland Ramsey, a medical officer, was also now housed in six block. Number three block held only three Americans, all the others were British. The commander of number three block was Brigadier General Donald Hobson. Also in three block was Major Nigel Loring, a Canadian who later came to number six block. The medical officer in three block was Colonel K. P. MacKenzie. Colonel MacKenzie would later offer a tremendous service to some American fliers.

Bombing raids were increasing. American bombers were coming from India and China and would usually appear over Rangoon around noon. The prisoners would stand out in the compound yard and watch them make their bombing run toward the docks. We would cheer like kids at a football game. When the anti-aircraft fire would be heavy we would yell, "Get out! Get out!" I would often wonder who was manning those bombers.

After I returned to Kentucky following the war, I learned that Jeff Garrott, a friend from high school and a teammate on the Mayfield High School football team, had flown with the 308th Bomb Group and participated in some of those bombing runs over Rangoon. Jeff was forced to bail out on one mission but returned safely to his base. I often kidded him that he escaped just so he could come back and drop more bombs on me.

Near the end of 1943, Major Warners' B-24 crew was shot down, captured and brought into solitary confinement. They remained there five days without medical treatment before Colonel MacKenzie, the medical officer from three black, was finally allowed to see them.

He was greeted by a horrible sight. The men had been crawling around on the dirt floor on their hand and knees for three days, without food or water. Except for the mouth and nose, their heads were completely bandaged. They were unable to use their hands. They could not feed themselves, and since their eyes were bandaged they were unable to see. All the men suffered from burns on their necks and faces. These burns had been dressed with a Vaseline-type substance on top of which sheets of grease-proof paper and layers of gauze had been placed. The grease-proof paper had been ineffective and the cream had soaked through the bandages. The result was a horrible coagulated mass of sand and dirt and grease that covered the necks and heads of these American airmen. MacKenzie was allowed to exam the men but was not permitted to speak with them.

Colonel MacKenzie said that the first man that he examined was in a state of collapse from the spread of infection. He clearly did not have long to live. MacKenzie turned his attention to the other men then insisted to the Japanese that he needed help from Major Ramsey. The British doctor was summoned.

MacKenzie and Ramsey examined the men and quickly reached the same conclusion: to have a chance of survival they should be taken immediately to a hospital in Rangoon for proper medical care. This message was relayed to the commandant, who refused. Ramsey and MacKenzie did their best to clean and dress the men's wounds. But once they had removed the filthy bandages, the two medical officers were greeted with yet another horror. The men were infested with maggots. In the days before MacKenzie was allowed to see the airmen, the prisoners in number six block had heard the men screaming and pleading to "stop sticking those sticks in my eyes" and "get those sticks out of my ears." But the pain wasn't coming from sticks. It was caused by maggots.

MacKenzie and Ramsey requested to commandant that they be allowed to take these men to number three and number six block, respectively, so they would receive some level of care. This time the commandant agreed.

Of the three men MacKenzie transported to number three block, one died the first night. The second man lived for about 48 hours, displaying tremendous courage to the end although one eye socket had been found filled with maggots when his head bandages were removed. The third man - Sergeant Daily - was a burly American who, amazingly, completely recovered. He was later moved to six block.

The two airmen Major Ramsey brought to number six block from solitary later died in the prison's make-shift hospital.

The Japanese allowed no lights. But during the daylight hours Don Ramsey, with the aid of Lt. Humphrey, would take the two crippled American fliers outside and remove the maggots from their sores. At night we took turns sitting up with them. I was with one of the men the night he died. He had been the bombardier on Warner's crew. He wasn't rational and talked about "a horrible sight" and "how terrible it was." He finally breathed a last breath and was gone.

The Japanese paid the POW officers each month. Officers were paid according to their rank, although the Japanese deducted some of the money from each officer. A reason for the deduction was not given. The officers used their money to buy some duck eggs or maybe some tobacco or jerky. A first lieutenant like Cotton would get about $7.00 or $9.00 per month. The money did not go far. It took $1.00 to buy a duck egg, and $1.00 to buy a cigar. But still the officers were paid. Cotton would buy what food and other items that he could and share them with his men. I'm sure some other officers did the same thing for the other enlisted men.

By spring 1944, a steady stream of officers and enlisted men were arriving at the prison. Cotton and Humphreys suggested to the American officers that they each donate a part of their monthly pay to buy food for the enlisted men. This was an enormous help. Each enlisted man could now expect to get a couple of duck eggs or other extra food item. From a prisoners' perspective, the best rank to hold was that of a second lieutenant. A second lieutenant wasn't expected to know very much, but he would be paid along with the other officers. Also, a second lieutenant - like all officers - was not required to labor on the work parties. One officer did accompany each work party as the officer in charge.

Officers and enlisted men were also separated at meal time. Cooked rice was then brought to each group in large buckets. In the officers' cell the highest ranking man would divide the rice. The noncommissioned officer in charge would divide the rice for the enlisted men. Each man would place his mess pan on the floor around the rice bucket to be filled.

Distributing the food was one of my jobs, and I think it was one of the hardest jobs in the prison. All the men would crowd around the bucket to see that the rice was divided evenly. There was never enough food and everyone left as they had arrived: hungry.

In March 1944 I was suffering from scabies, had beri-beri in my ankles, and had developed some deep jungle sores on my left leg. Captain B. N. Sudan of the British Army Medical Corps would often ask Lieutenant Cotton about my condition and send something for me.

We had a great deal of sickness in six block. A group of six people, including myself, were sent to three block for treatment by Colonel MacKenzie. The overall treatment of the men began to improve slightly. This was probably a result of the increasing allied successes in Burma. Some of the work parties also found some copper sulfate. In its crystalline form copper sulfate is blue. This gives it the common name, blue stone. The work detail managed to smuggle some blue stone back into the prison. MacKenzie had the stone crushed to a fine powder. He would then dissolve it with water and use it for treating jungle sores. It was painful (copper sulfate causes an intense burning sensation) but effective. This treatment probably saved many lives.

When moved to three block, I was suffering from three jungle sores on my left leg. Each was slightly larger than a quarter and close enough together to be covered by the palm of a hand. MacKenzie was a fine physician and saved many lives, as did Captain Sudan. But MacKenzie had a habit of telling the men that there was no such thing as pain. At one point, the colonel was suffering from scabies. He was walking in the courtyard and met Sergeant Bud Crostic. MacKenzie said, "Good morning sergeant." Then added, "These scabies are bloody painful." Crostic answered him immediately, "Colonel there is no such thing as pain." MacKenzie simply looked up at Crostic, grinned, and went on his way.

This is how MacKenzie treated jungle sores. He would cover the tip of a bamboo stick with cloth, knock away the scab, then swab the pus until the sore began to bleed. He would then take a strong solution of copper sulfate and clean the infected tissue. This was done twice a day. The blue stone burned, but it did help the sores. While MacKenzie was treating my leg I didn't complain because I knew he was not only trying to save my leg, but also my life.

Like many of the men, I continued to suffer from dysentery and beri-beri. Lieutenant Cotton instructed the cook house to make a couple of small flat cakes from raw bran and water. These were then baked. They were supposed to provide some vitamin B-2 to help the beri-beri. Eventually, though, starvation and disease will cause a man to lose his appetite. In the prison camp this was called "getting off your rice." When a man did this it was difficult to recover. By this time I was off my rice. Most of my friends would try to get me to eat, but they were kind in their approach. Not Bud Crostic.

Crostic would say, "Don't eat your food, I don't care. Give it to me. You're going to die anyway." This would make me mad, and I'd eat a little more which was what he wanted, although I didn't know it at the time.

After a few weeks, my jungle sores began to heal. As they improved, Colonel MacKenzie would decrease the concentration of the copper sulfate solution. All the time I remained in three block MacKenzie treated me twice a day. When I returned to six block in May 1944 my jungle sores were almost healed.

By mid-1944 all the American POWs were in six block. Nigel Loring, a British major who had been in number three block, returned to six block with us. He became the block commander.

Six block had been under the command of a British captain who didn't do much for organization. Basically, each man had been left to fend for himself. This seemed to compound the filth, sickness and death in the block. When Loring took command he made several changes. He was not hesitant to argue with the Japanese and constantly made requests to improve conditions.

One thing Loring did was assign a detail to clean up the compound. He asked for volunteers to empty and clean the wooden box latrines. This is a filthy job which no one wanted. To get volunteers

Loring ordered that the men on this detail be given one and one half rations of rice with each meal. He also gave the cooks an extra half ration of rice. This was done to prevent the men in the cook house from stealing rice.

When Loring came from three block he brought with him an English barber who had a straight razor, a pair of scissors and a razor strap. No one seemed to know where he got these items. Loring ordered each man to get a shave and a haircut at least once a month. The man receiving the shave or haircut also had to give the barber a cigarette, which could be made by using some ingenuity. The barber also didn't go out on work details. His work was cutting hair.

Major Loring moved the hospital to a room inside the main building and converted the old hospital building - which had open air slat walls - into a cook house. He also obtained more firewood which consequently allowed us to sometimes have tea during the day. This was a major improvement. Major Loring was not liked by everyone. But his efforts lowered the death rate and saved lives.

Occasionally the Japanese would slaughter a cow. They always came to six block for Major Gene Lutz, who was an American fighter pilot. The Japanese would make Lutz and two or three other men butcher the animal then sometimes give us the head, blood and entrails. On rare occasions we also got a small piece of the meat.

My jungle sores had much improved. But when moved back to number six block I was still suffering from beri-beri and dysentery. Lieutenant Cotton had an opportunity to see Captain Sudan, who always asked about me. Cotton told him I again had beri-beri and that it didn't look good. Captain Sudan told Cotton that he would go to the guard house to see the Japanese and while there steal some vitamin B pills. Sudan managed to get the pills and that night, at a pre-arranged spot, threw them over our compound wall to Cotton. I was told to chew, not swallow, them at the rate of one or two per day as long as they lasted. They worked, and the beri-beri improved.

Captain Sudan did much for me but he also helped many other men in the camp. Chinese Major General H. C. Chi sent a letter to the English Brigadier General Hobson in number three block to express his appreciation for Captain B. N. Sudan and his services to the Chinese prisoners.

I cannot offer enough praise for Captain Sudan. He went far beyond the call of duty not only for me but also for all the Chinese, Indians, English and other Americans in the camp. Although he was a frail man he had extraordinary stamina and held up well under the rigors of the camp. After liberation, I visited him in Calcutta in an Indian hospital. At that time he appeared tired and ill. General Chi's letter said:

To Brigadier General Hobson. To Captain B. N. Sudan, B.A.M.C.

March 4, 1944.

Dear Sir:

I beg to inform you that for more than six months our sick men, with the permission of the Japanese, have been placed under the medical care of four British medical officers: Captains Sudan, K. Pillay, Thomas and Rao, all Indian officers in the British Army. Among them Captain B. N. Sudan's services have been especially valuable to us. During this period we have not had a single death and three of our soldiers were virtually snatched from the very jaws of death. All through the efforts of that good officer. In consideration of the difficulties imposed upon by the Japanese and the regrettable lack of medical facilities at present he has certainly done a great deal.

It would indeed be ungrateful on my part not to acknowledge the very considerable service he had rendered to us. It is therefore only just for me to bring his excellent service to notice of the most senior British officer here and to express our appreciation and thanks thereby.

I will be ready and only to glad to bear testimony to the above statement when called upon to do so at any time after the war if I am lucky enough to survive it.

I beg to remain respectfully yours,

H. C. Chi, Major General, Chinese

When the British and American working parties would form each morning outside our compounds we would often hear a cheerful "good morning." This greeting came from General Chi, who had been "reduced" in rank to private by the Japanese.

General Chi told us if any Chinese or Japanese newspapers were smuggled into the camp he could interpret it then share the news with the British and American prisoners. He had been educated in both America and Japan and could speak several languages.

General Chi had absolutely refused to help the Japanese. This action which resulted in his immediate deposit in solitary confinement. He was visited by the Kempeitai, tortured, beaten, and at various times denied food and water. Through it all he never lost his composure or confidence and always managed to have a smile for his fellow prisoners.

The Chinese Nationalist Government had been driven back to Chungking in 1942. Japan has set up a puppet government in China under Wang Ching Wei. This leadership was directed by the Japanese at Nanking. The Japanese occasionally sent officers from Nanking to the Rangoon prison to try to recruit General Chi. He was considered by the Japanese to be a highly important prisoner. (It was widely rumored among the prisoners that General Chi had married into the family of Madam Chaing Kai-Shek.)

One day a delegation from the Japanese-supported Chinese puppet government arrived at the jail. After meeting with the commandant they went to see General Chi. They looked very official in their crisp, clean Chinese National uniforms. They expressed horror at seeing a senior officer like General Chi, who they claimed to be a fellow officer and countryman, in jail. They insisted that the general be supplied with a bath and proper dress and then accompany them outside the prison for a meal.

General Chi enjoyed it all immensely. But then the time came to discuss the real reason for their visit. The head of the delegation said that they had come to take General Chi back to Nanking to participate in the new government of China. They always referred to the Japanese as a "benevolent people." General Chi was told he would be required to sign a certificate declaring his good intentions and behavior toward the new government, after which he would be a free man.

The general flatly refused, although he explained that he had enjoyed the meal and the outing. It was probably incomprehensible to the members of the delegation that the general would miss this opportunity for freedom and elect to remain in the prison.

General Chi was returned to solitary and, we later learned, was subjected to additional torture. We now rarely saw the general; the Japanese kept him isolated most of the time. He would continue to send messages whenever possible. They were always optimistic.

Shortly after he was released from solitary and returned to his compound, General Chi was stabbed while lying in his bunk. He was attacked by one of his own soldiers who had switched his allegiance in support of the Japanese-backed Chinese government.

General Chi received a deep stab would to his lower abdomen - a wound that probably would not have been fatal if given prompt and proper medical care. Of course, this was not available. The afternoon following the attack Colonel MacKenzie was summoned and an interpreter told him General Chi was wounded in the liver. The Japanese wanted Colonel MacKenzie to operate on the general. MacKenzie suggested that General Chi be taken to a local or military hospital for surgery, but the Japanese refused. MacKenzie then operated on the Chinese general.

The next morning the medical officer was shown a dressing that had been removed from General Chi's wound. What he saw was not good. The wound had pierced the bowel. MacKenzie knew surgery would be required immediately if the general was to have a chance of survival. MacKenzie again suggested that the general be taken for proper medical care but the Japanese again refused. The British doctor agreed to perform the surgery.

The operation took place within the hour. Major Ramsey again assisted MacKenzie, as he had when the two medical officers treated the five American airmen in solitary confinement. The Japanese had produced two pair of rubber gloves and two surgical gowns for the doctors. MacKenzie explained to General Chi that he and Ramsey would do their best. After the crude operation MacKenzie told the general that he was sorry that he couldn't do more for him. General Chi said that he understood and was then taken away by the Japanese.

He died about 36 hours later.

Chapter 13

The Light of the Moon

As late as mid-1944 the Japanese apparently still thought that they could win the war. Treatment at the camp was brutal. Perhaps they did not believe they would have to answer for their actions. The compound death rates remained high. We would sometimes lose two or three men a day in six block alone.

It became a daily struggle for survival. Each man believed we would be liberated but, of course, no one knew when. No one displayed a self-pitying attitude. That would have only caused problems. A man had only to look around him to witness other POWs in worse condition than he.

At night we would sometimes come outside into the courtyard and look up at the moon. You'd be surprised by the amount of comfort it delivers. Watching the moon was the only link that we had with our friends and family back home. They did not know our whereabouts. They didn't even know if we were alive. It was comforting to know that we could see the same heavenly object that they could see. We got a great of comfort from knowing that same moon could be seen over Kentucky or Missouri or Illinois or California or wherever a man was from.

We were hungry and suffering from various diseases. I believe that we probably needed medicine as badly as we needed food. If the allies knew our whereabouts, we thought, maybe they would send a plane with a drop of food and medical supplies. We knew the Japanese would get most of the supplies, but if one package got through, that would be enough.

Today, when media brings us reports of people in desperate need of both food and medicine someone will say, "Well, there's so much corruption the people probably won't get a third of anything we send." Maybe not. But the one-third or one-fourth or one-fifth that they might get would be the most wonderful thing in the world to the people in need. That's how we felt. When food is sent to starving people today profiteers and thieves and corrupt governments may take some of it but what gets through will feed and help a few hungry or sick people. If one-tenth gets through it's worth the effort.

A popular phrase related that God helps those who help themselves. The men inside the Rangoon jail did try to help themselves. But they also helped others. As a Rangoon POW you had to concentrate on surviving and not on the surrounding conditions. Some of the prisoners in Rangoon withstood the torture and starvation and ill treatment surprisingly well. A few, though, quickly become depressed and eventually lost their will to fight.

Other men gained strength from their Christian belief. We had no minister or priest to conduct formal religious service. It was not permitted by the Japanese, although many men would hold a prayer time and religious services.

A few of the men questioned how God could permit such cruelty and the deaths of so many young people. We wondered how the Japanese could be so successful fighting thousands of miles from their homeland. These were only a couple of questions that we asked ourselves. But the men who held to a strong religious faith knew the answers. It was truly a period of darkness. No matter how tough a man thought he was; regardless of the type of life he had led; there was only one place to turn. And that was to God.

Chapter 14

Hope

By late 1944 and early 1945 our treatment improved as the war swung heavily in favor of the allies. Hopes were lifted when conditions improved.

By the end of 1944 hundreds of men had died. No one knows how many. New prisoners were still arriving almost daily, most of whom were airmen.

Perry Marshall, Don Davis, Bill Thomas and I had become very good friends. I slept next to Marshall and Davis, and they noticed that my dysentery was not improving. Davis had managed to get three sulfur pills from the escape kit in his parachute. He had managed to sneak these into the prison. Like me, Davis had suffered from dysentery while in solitary. But he had taken two of these sulfur pills and dysentery stopped. Davis kept his last pill in case he fell ill again. Now, he sought Perry's opinion about giving this last sulfur pill to me. Perry pointed out that Davis could very easily need himself. They still had no way of knowing how long they would be in prison and sickness was common. "True," Davis said, "But I know John needs it and he needs it now." He gave me his final tablet and this single sulfur pill stopped my dysentery.

Don Davis did become ill before we were liberated but he survived and made it home. He died of cancer in 1988. I have always believed that if he had not shared his medicine with me I might not have survived the camp.

I got some blue stone solution to clean scabies on my legs, arms, chest and back. I was trying to rub the sores when an English lad came up and said, "Let me help you with those sores." Knowing that no one really wanted to do this because scabies were contagious I said, "No thanks. I could do it by myself." He said, "But you can't reach the ones on your back. Give me that cloth." I gave it to him, and he washed my sores for me. The man's name was Leo Frank. He was a British commando from London. I'll never forget him for that favor.

In 1989, after the Ex-Rangoon POW Association in the United States had been organized, a list of member names and addresses were sent to the association that was formed in England. I got a letter from Leo Frank. He ask if I was the same Sergeant Boyd whom he had helped his wash sores in the Rangoon Prison Camp. It was great to hear from him and we've corresponded several times since.

By mid-1944 my health was beginning to improve for the first time since I had been captured. I didn't really realize how sick and badly injured I'd been until I started to improve. Then, in July 1944, a cholera epidemic broke out in the prison. It could have easily killed everyone in the compound, prisoners and captors. Colonel MacKenzie gives this account of the Rangoon cholera epidemic in his book *Operation Rangoon Jail.*

If cholera had obtained a substantial hold in Rangoon Jail it would have eliminated the prisoners just as straw before a prairie fire. It would have been little compensation, but it would also have eliminated the Japs as well.

A soldier came back from Rangoon with his working party one evening complaining of a terrible, unnatural, hunger. He ate his supper that night then had some of his comrades rations as well. That night he began suffering severe abdominal pain and attacks of acute diarrhea. In the early morning he soiled his own blanket and the floor and the blankets of two other men as they tried to get him to the latrine. Colonel MacKenzie was summoned and was struck by the man's visible dehydration.

MacKenzie asked if he had eaten something while on the work party. The soldier said no. The medical officer then had the sick man moved to the hospital. There MacKenzie told the men that this soldier was suffering from some type of choleric diarrhea and that he should be closely watched. He was given a bunk among the beri-beri patients. When MacKenzie visited the six block hospital ward he found the patients close to this man suffering from severe abdominal cramps, vomiting and involuntary liquid stool.

MacKenzie immediately informed the Japanese that cholera had broken out. These men were isolated in a separate room but the prisoners were helpless to properly deal with a cholera outbreak. The hospital room was cleared and disinfected with a chloride and lime solution. MacKenzie asked that 20 cholera outfits be sent to the prison. He knew there was a very real danger that the American and British prisoners in six block would be eliminated by cholera. The Japanese refused MacKenzie's request.

Major Ramsey had the cholera patients moved into a building prisoner's called the "candle factory." This was where we made candles. Once the men were isolated there was little to do except wait and hope. We were extremely fortunate. No other cases of cholera occurred in the compound.

Sergeant John Leisure, my engineer, was one of the men stricken with cholera. He died in the candle factory. Major Loring had asked for a volunteer to go to isolation to care for the men. Private Brown, an English medical orderly, volunteered for this duty. He also died from the disease. When Major Loring announced Private Brown's death he said, "If I live to get back, I will see that this man is recognized for what he has done." I hope that he did.

During the epidemic the Japanese came into number six block in white coats, white gloves, rubber boots and masks. They vaccinated the men in six block, although I do not know what kind of vaccination they used. The Japanese also weighted us for the first time. I was weighted at 97 pounds. John Leisure weighted 87 pounds when he died. The big engineer's normal weight was about 190 pounds.

The cholera epidemic ran its course in 14 days. We lost 10 men to the disease.

By August 1944 northern Burma had begun to fall to the allies. About the same time both the food and treatment inside the jail improved. My physical condition also improved and I joined work parties outside the prison.

I was on one work party to St. Mary's School. This had been a high school before the war but the Japanese were using it for offices and officer's housing. One of our jobs was to dig an air raid shelter under one of the houses. While on this job one of our men found some canned dog biscuits. They were stale and hard as bone. But they did taste good. Also, while on this work party, we heard our first news of the war in more than a year.

We were working around a house quartering several Japanese officers. Through an open window we could hear a radio playing Indian music. The music stopped and the announcer, in crisp English, said, "This is All India Radio, British Broadcasting Company, New Delhi, India, and this is the latest news today." The announcer said the allies had landed at Normandy had advanced to within 50 miles of Paris, encountering only light resistance. Then the radio was turned off.

Our collective hearts leapt into our throats. The joy this news brought was almost overwhelming. Even now, more than 50 years later, I can still feel the excitement of hearing that radio broadcast. Our main concern since capture was: how long would this war last and could we stay alive until its end? We now had proof the allies were coming. We couldn't wait to get back to the compound and tell our comrades. This was not a rumor. It was not a guess. I heard this on the radio myself!

Judson College was in the northwest section of the city. When the

Japanese took Rangoon they converted this school into their headquarters. This is where Leisure and I were first questioned when we were brought to Rangoon. In Fall of 1944, work parties began digging an air raid shelter at the college. A large Japanese sergeant supervised this project. He weighted about 225 pounds and had been a professional wrestler in Tokyo. We gave him the name "Bulldozer."

The shelter measured about 30 ft. by 40 ft. and was nine to 10 ft. deep. We dug with picks and shovels, carrying the dirt out of the pit bamboo baskets. A long timber was placed against the wall of the pit and two men would walk up this timber carrying a basket of dirt. We would often have to bail out gallons of water before beginning work. All the time we were working, the Japanese guards were shouting at us or beating us because we weren't working fast enough, or because we had slipped and fallen, or for some other silly reason.

After the pit was dug we went to the docks and got some 10 in. x 10 in. teakwood timbers 18 to 20 feet long. These were used to build a frame inside the pit. Then a layer of 10" x 10" timbers were placed a top the shelter. Crushed rock and gravel were added, then a second layer of timbers were applied to the roof. Then a mound of dirt about eight feet high was added. It was then sodded and camouflaged. It was a solid shelter but I doubt it would have survived a direct hit.

We worked throughout the day except for a short break to eat the rice that we had brought with us. Each day while we were eating, the Japanese would bring out their garbage from the noon meal. The orderly would dump it not far from where we were eating our lunch. We would then rush to salvage what food we could from the scraps. The Japanese thought this was very funny.

This caused me to remember my arrival in India. When we dumped the leftovers from our mess kits the natives would pick through the garbage. Little did I know that within a couple of years I would be doing the same thing. An experience like that changes your perspective on many things.

The work on the air raid shelter was hard. I remembered movies that I had seen depicting enslaved people from Biblical times and thought it strange that human behavior had not changed. I was also amazed by the volume of work that could be generated by sick men.

The Japanese were in a terrible hurry to complete the bomb shelter. The guards were always trying to hurry us in our work. A Japanese civilian worked at the headquarters building and saw the treatment that we were receiving. He requested that four or five of the obviously ill prisoners do some work at the officers boat club and grounds. He later said that he made the request to get us away from the harsh treatment we were receiving while working on the air raid shelter. He said he was sorry for this. I was one of the men allowed to go on the boat club work party and I was glad to be relieved from the air raid shelter job. This Japanese civilian talked with us two or three times. He always wanted to know how we thought the war was going. He was a good man. I hope he returned safely to Tokyo.

There was also an English Welchman who worked with us at Judson College. He had quite a sense of humor and was a morale builder. His name was Tish Morgan and he kept our spirits up when times were tough. It was about a 20 minute ride from the prison to Judson College. When we would start back to the jail, Morgan would shout, "Men, are they taking it out of us?" We would all shout, "No. No. No." Then he would start singing:

> Bless 'em all. Bless 'em all. Bless 'em all.
> The long, the short and the tall.
> There'll be no promotions this side of the ocean,
> So cheer up my lads. Bless 'em all.

This would make the Japanese angry. They'd stop the truck and start to bash us with their rifle butts or sticks, whacking any man they could reach.

We would stop singing and the truck would start rolling again. After a few minutes Morgan would say, "Men, are they taking it out of us?" We would all shout, "No! No! No!" And he'd start the singing again:

> Pack up your troubles in an old knit bag
> And smile, smile, smile.
> What's the use in worrying?
> It never was worthwhile.

The Japanese would stop the truck and bash us again and we would stop singing. Then the truck would roll and Morgan would start the same routine, usually with another song:

> Roll out the barrel.
> We'll have a barrel of fun.
> Roll out the barrel.
> We've got the Japs on the run.

This would continue three or four times until we got to the prison.

At night we would listen for the air raid sirens or for the sounds of approaching aircraft. We would think about homes and our families and friends and what they might be doing. We also had a British soldier in our room, Private Yates, who had a wonderful singing voice. He was a shy man who didn't like to sing in public. But at night, in the dark, he would serenade us. One of the things the men enjoyed most was to hear Yates sing. He would even take requests: *White Cliffs of Dover, White Christmas, Blue Moon, When the Lights Come on Again all over the World, Moonlight Serenade, Moonlight Becomes You, Moon River, The Last Time I Saw Paris* and others.

It always helped. When the chips were down Yate's singing would re-kindle our hope and encouragement.

Chapter 15

War Crimes

While on the work parties we could tell that conditions in Rangoon were changing. On one occasion, at Judson College a Japanese officer came out and talked to us. He asked us how long we thought the war would last. We told him we didn't know, of course, but we hoped it would not last much longer. We were interested in his opinion of the war so we let him do most of the talking. He agreed that it would not last much longer. He did not say that Japan would win the war. He did say that Japan had not wanted war but was forced into it when the United States cut off trade. He was friendly; his demeanor was not at all like we had experience only a few months earlier. Things were changing.

By the end of November 1944 the air raid shelter at Judson College had been completed. The air raids over Rangoon were also increasing. Most working parties had stopped going outside the prison.

One day I was working with a small group of prisoners in the Japanese vegetable garden planted next to the main prison wall. We heard air raid sirens, but by that time, the planes were already over the prison. It was a large formation of 20 to 25 bombers. They generated a tremendous roar. They were larger than any airplane we had every seen. These were B-29s, the new muscle of the American Air Force, although we didn't know it at the time. The big bombers flew over the jail and hit the docks, dropping their loads simultaneously. They really shook the ground.

The guard who was with us in the garden was terrified; almost in panic. He pushed me against the wall, raised his gun butt and called me "no good American fly boy." I quickly told him, "No. No. English ground soldier. English ground soldier" I don't think I convinced him I was English, but he didn't hit me with the rifle.

On December 14, 1944 the B-29s were again bombing the Rangoon docks. We were in the six block courtyard watching the raid. We later learned that the target was a bridge south of the city, but it was socked in so they turned to the docks as a secondary target. The planes approached from the south at about 20,000 feet when apparently a bomb with an instantaneous fuse hit another bomb. The explosion caused four planes to crash. A fifth plane had three engines out, one engine on fire and one wing and the bomb bay compartment aflame. The 12-man crew still managed to bail out.

Master Sergeant Richard Montgomery was one of the men who escaped from the crippled aircraft. But Montgomery nearly had his hand severed in the explosion. He and two crew mates made it to a small Burmese village where they were handed over to the Japanese.

The Japanese took Montgomery and his crew mates to a police station where they were forced to stand for more than six hours. Montgomery was badly in need of medical attention as his crew mates repeatedly told the Japanese. Their complaints brought only physical abuse. Later, however, a Japanese doctor did sever Montgomery's hand and bandage the arm.

The next morning they were brought to the Rangoon prison. Two of the men were placed in the general compound, but Montgomery was put in solitary confinement.

The prison interrogator told Colonel MacKenzie that the Japanese medical lieutenant from Rangoon who visited the jail on occasion wished to see him. The Japanese lieutenant wanted MacKenzie to help him with a surgical procedure. MacKenzie reluctantly agreed then asked to see the patient. But the lieutenant refused and MacKenzie was dismissed.

About two hours later the colonel was again summoned. This time, he was brought to the water tower which was in the center of the prison. There he found the Japanese medical officer had assembled a crude operating room and a waiting patient. MacKenzie later learned this was Master Sergeant Montgomery.

Montgomery's arm was filthy and infected. The bone was protruding from the wound and he was suffering from intense nerve pain. MacKenzie could see that he had only two choices. One was to operate high on the forearm; The other was to remove the limb at the elbow. The surgical tools supplied to MacKenzie included; four scalpels, six forceps, two hypodermic needles and a saw - not a surgical saw but an ordinary butcher's saw - along with a few strands of horsehair. Given the tools at hand he chose to remove the arm at the elbow and avoid using the saw.

MacKenzie explained to Montgomery that he was trying to save his life and would be as gentle as possible. The Japanese produced some numbing painkiller which was injected into Montgomery's arm as the doctor worked. The operation took about an hour and a half, after which Montgomery, with help from two other prisoners, walked back to his block. MacKenzie was returned to three block. This was the last time MacKenzie saw Sergeant Montgomery, although the American airman survived and was liberated May 3, 1945.

I saw Montgomery several years later at an air base in Florida. He helped me secure a new post assignment.

MacKenzie would also hear from Montgomery. After MacKenzie had returned to England he read a column in the *England Daily Telegraph* about artificial limbs. The story explained how some servicemen who had suffered loss of limbs in World War II were being fitted with artificial limbs and had re-entered the service. The news column told the story of a Master Sergeant Richard Montgomery and how he had rejoined the Army Air Force as a radio operator after being fitted with an artificial arm. The story told how British medical officer K. P. MacKenzie had removed Montgomery's arm in the Rangoon Prison Camp. The article said: "The sergeant has never seen Colonel MacKenzie since Rangoon was re-taken from the Japanese in May 1945. He speaks of him with the highest admiration and affection, however, and would like to get in touch with him. Perhaps Colonel MacKenzie will read this column . . ."

MacKenzie did read it of course, and the two men were reunited by letter.

* * *

In 1946 an article appeared in the *Chicago Sun* by Eddy Voherty. The story was told by Edward J. Leary, who had been a captain in an army intelligence section. Leary assisted in tracking and locating war criminals. The story in part read:

> . . .23 men, Japanese army officers and prison guards who beat and murdered American soldiers were rounded up by (Leary) and placed on trial. Some have been hanged and others will be hanged soon. 'I didn't do it all by myself,' Leary said. 'I had the help of Technical Sergeant Harry Suzakawa. . .
> He at present (1946) serving as court interpreter in Rangoon at the war trials. Without his aid and that of other American-Japanese soldiers I might be still looking for most of these men.'

Leary, a former reporter for the *Chicago Sun,* revealed to the public some of the horrifying stories the Rangoon prisoners knew first hand. He said some of the Rangoon prisoners had given him a list of names of their more brutal captors. In some cases the guards had nicknames like "Tarzan" "Nose" and "Hollywood." Leary and his men were especially interested in a guard the prisoners referred to as 'Tarzan." The Rangoon POWs reported that he was particularly vicious. They learned that his real name was Kooigetsu Ueno and he was a superior private in the Japanese army. He admitted that he was a guard at the Rangoon Central Jail and was in charge of the solitary confinement block. He also admitted to being called "Tarzan" by some of the prisoners and that he had beaten every American in his charge.

Ueno was sentenced to death by hanging but this was later commuted to life in prison.

Leary also investigated the January 1, 1945 severe beating by drunken Japanese soldiers of all the American prisoners who were still in solitary confinement. Some of the men died after they were refused medical treatment. The Japanese medical officer who refused to treat the men was Lieutenant Akio Onishi. He was found after the war and made a confession stating that the officer in charge, Captain Motozo Tazumi, told him to treat the American airmen as criminals and not as prisoners of war.

Another particularly brutal episode uncovered by Leary during the war trials in Rangoon involved an Indian native named Ratnun Burai.

Burai was a British subject but was employed as a spy by the American army. One of his duties was to install radios in enemy territory - a job that required being dropped behind enemy lines by parachute. Burai was betrayed by a friend (who was later killed by the British) and taken to the New Law Courts building in Rangoon. Each morning he was taken from his cell and questioned about the radio code and each morning he was returned to his cell unconscious. This continued for two months. Although Burai was beaten and tortured repeatedly he refused to help the Japanese. He died with his loyalty intact.

Chapter 16

A Trip to Saigon

In February 1945 Lieutenant Goad, Sergeant Marshall and Sergeant Hubbard were taken by the Japanese from the Rangoon Central Jail to Saigon. Their mission: to fly a B-24 for the Japanese.

Sergeant Perry Marshall tells the story:

> The Japanese interpreter came with some guards to our compound and called for Lieutenant Goad, Sergeant Hubbard and me. Goad was a B-24 pilot, Hubbard was a flight engineer and I, too, was a flight engineer. We were told we were going to take a trip but, of course, we didn't have anything to pack - not even a tooth brush.

> They took us to the airport in Rangoon where we spent the night trying to get some sleep on wood benches or the concrete floor. By sunrise the Japanese were up and we were taken out to an area close to where the planes were parked. The twin engine planes were covered with brush and other camouflage materials. The Japanese uncovered and loaded one of the planes. The pilot and crew arrived, climbed aboard and started the plane. One engine ran very rough. The pilot jumped out and began shouting at the crew chief and actually beat him up while making him stand at attention.

> The gear was unloaded and re-loaded into the other plane. The pilot came over to us, pulled his pistol and fired three shots over our heads while he lectured us, all the while making us stand at attention. The interpreter said if we made any trouble on the plane he would shoot us, and I believed him.

> They took us to Saigon and housed us on the third floor of a wooden building. The room had three straw mattresses and mosquito netting. We also had a place to bathe with soap and towels. They gave us shorts and a shirt and were even allowed to eat in their mess hall, although, of course, after their people were fed. Compared to Rangoon this was high living.

> The place we were housed was near a Japanese office building. The Japanese would come over daily to talk to us, usually one at a time. They were very mysterious about why we were there. They finally told us they had in their possession a B-24 that they thought could be flown, and we would be the ones to fly it.

From our room we were near an open window of this office building and could hear a daily phone conversation about us. We always referred to as the 'three Americans.' The phone conversations and visits to our room continued for several days. Lieutenant Goad (the pilot) told Hubbard and I that whatever we did, all three of us would make the decision together.

We told the Japanese that we did not want to fly their B-24. We knew without question the we would be flying against our own army. We decided that if we were forced to fly the plane we'd take it up then crash it in order to destroy it.

After about 10 days in Saigon the Japanese decided to forget the B-24 and we were sent back to Rangoon, but that meant another ride on one of their twin-engine outfits. This time when we got to the landing strip the Japanese ground crew had the plugs out of the engines and were scrubbing them with toothbrushes and gasoline

We did make it back to Rangoon and even got to keep the shorts and shirts. Although living was much better in Saigon we were glad to be away from that place and back in Rangoon and with our friends.

Chapter 17

The End is Near

By the spring 1945 it was clear that the end of the war was approaching. The bombing raids were increasing and the docks were a mass of rubble. A few guards had begun to ask the prisoners what we thought would happen to them if the American's arrived. We told them that if they arrived and found that we were being treated by the rules of the Geneva Convention everything would be fine. But if they found us starving and beaten, then there was no telling what they would do. The guards acted like they were kidding. We knew they were worried.

On March 22 a wave of B-29s approached from the north. After dropping their bombs they flew directly over the prison. This was the first time the bombers had flown over the jail since the Japanese made Lieutenant Cotton go on the radio the previous year and announce that POWs were being held in the Rangoon Central Jail.

It was about this time that the Japanese gave us three head of cattle. They provided a welcome addition to our diet. For the first time in months we sat down and ate our fill.

There was no longer any apparent reason for the 5:00 a.m. roll calls, but they continued. In late April the Japanese issued some new mess kits. Then, to everyone's surprise, we were issued soap for the first time. There was a good deal of activity around the guard house and gun shots could be heard in the city. The Japanese also informed us that President Roosevelt had died.

Colonel MacKenzie, who had been in the Rangoon jail since 1942, remarked that he had a feeling things were coming to a head, but for some reason he might not survive.

A state of collapse seemed to be developing around the guard room. Around 11:00 a.m. on April 24, 200 of the prisoners were ordered to stand by for a march. Brigadier General Hobson was notified that all British and American prisoners were to be moved at 4:00 p.m. that day. This was disappointing news to all the prisoners. Allied fighters were now over the city almost constantly. It was obvious that the end was very near. Everyone wished to remain in the jail and be liberated.

During the next few hours the Japanese changed their orders several times. It was finally decided that 76 American and 365 British POWs would make the march - to where, though, no one knew. All other British and Americans were moved to number six block. I was one of the men left in the prison.

The atmosphere in the jail was now quiet. Strangely quiet. The Japanese were trying to force march the prisoners across the Burmese border into Thailand. But the widespread destruction caused by allied air strikes had left only one route open and that was north about 50 miles to Pegu then toward Singapore.

Each prisoner was given a Japanese outfit that included a soft cap, a pair of long white pants, some rubber shoes and a pair of khaki shorts. Some were given shirts. Each prisoner also received a cake of soap and a ration bag with a biscuit and a brown candy-like substance. Rations bags were issued to every third man.

Fifty men left with Major Loring's party and were to told to act as guards for the carts (some of the prisoners were pulling ammunition and supply carts). Several weeks later we learned that the original intent of the Japanese was to march the men through Siam up the China coast all the way to Japan. A strong Japanese advance party lead the troop and armed guards flanked the prisoners.

The men were forced to march at night. Allied air cover made it impossible to move during the day. Since the POWs were dressed in Japanese military clothes the fliers assumed they were Japanese soldiers. After three days the convoy was about four miles from Pegu. Some of the prisoners had begun to drop out of the line from hunger, fatigue or illness. The Japanese had also ordered the supply carts abandoned because they were slowing the march. By the fourth day the prisoners had gone without food for two days and had had no water for 24 hours. Colonel MacKenzie, the British medical officer who had helped so many men in the prison camp, was exhausted. He knew he was near the point of collapse. MacKenzie recalled this moment in his book, *Operation Rangoon*:

> Just as the convoy was moving off squadron leader Duckenfield and Captain Brown came up to me silently, they placed my arms around their shoulders and struggled forward bearing my entire body between them... When they faltered their place was taken by other men. We stopped every hour and at the end of each resting period there were always two men beside me to drag me along. For the last two hours the burden was borne by Sergeant Handsell and Sergeant Martin. They did more for me, as did the others, than any man had any reasonable right to request. They'd had no food themselves for 48 hours, and they were in a distressed condition.

They halted about 7:00 a.m. on April 29 at a small village on the Waupegu-Wau Road. Brigadier General Hobson was summoned to the Japanese commandant. A few minutes later Hobson called his men around him and announced, "We're free. We're free."

The Japanese commandant had told Hobson that they were abandoning the march and returning to Rangoon (although when the Japanese left them they moved north away from the city). Hobson had set up his headquarters in a small Burmese village hut. Later that day he was killed during a strafing attack by allied air crews.

Near dusk Major Lutz, Sergeant Lucus and Lieutenant Horner left in an attempt to get a message through to the American lines and let them know their location. They were successful in contacting a relief party and Lutz returned that night with the good news. Allied aircraft arrive soon and transported the prisoners to a field hospital near Calcutta.

The men who were left in the prison knew that the Japanese could hang on to Rangoon for months. We also knew that the allies faced a bloody, building-to-building, hand-to-hand fight, particularly if the Japanese could hold the city until the monsoons began. In London, Prime Minister Winston Churchill was demanding the capture of Rangoon at all cost because General Marshall had indicated that a good deal of American aid would be withdrawn once the monsoon started.

The British 14th Army had taken Meiktila (after the Japanese had mounted a fierce and bloody battle) and were moving toward Rangoon. However, at risk of being slowed by the coming monsoon, the allies began preparing for an amphibious assault up the Rangoon River.

The anticipated battle for Rangoon was avoided when Lieutenant General Kimura, who was commander-in-chief of the Japanese Burma Army and had been the vice minister of war, had other ideas. On April 22nd Kimura ordered that Rangoon be abandoned. The next day, he flew to Moulmein leaving what was left of his 100,000 man army to escape the on-coming British as best they could. This was so uncharacteristic of the Japanese fight-until-death tradition that the allied commanders didn't believe it. Their suspicions were supported when the advance units from the British 14th Army encountered stiff resistance near the outskirts of Pegu, about 50 miles north of Rangoon. Pegu had also been immediate destination of the prisoners who were marched from the Rangoon Jail. When the Japanese abandoned the march they had headed north toward Pegu where they may have encountered the advancing British.

Chapter 18

"Jap's Gone! Jap's Gone! Jap's Gone!"

After the 441 British and American prisoners left for the march to Pegu a muster was taken inside the jail. The remaining prisoners included 474 Indians, 123 British, 54 Chinese, 39 Americans, three Anglo-Burmese, two New Zealanders, one East African, one Canadian and one Australian. Lionel Hudson remained as ranking POW in charge. All the prisoners left behind were either sick, feeble or disabled. The Indians were in the best overall condition.

On the morning of April 30 we lined up in number six block for the 5:00 a.m. roll call. Major McLeod was in charge of officers in the first file. I had the American enlisted men in the next file. The British enlisted men made up the third group.

When the Japanese failed to appear McLeod sent a runner to the guard house. He came back shouting "Jap's gone! Jap's gone! Jap's gone!"

This was good news. We didn't expect it, but we were certainly glad to hear it.

The runner brought two notes from the guard house, both of which were neatly written in English. One was dated from Rangoon, 29 April 1945. It said:

> Gentlemen,
> Bravely you have come here opening prison. We have gone. Keeping you prisoners safely with Nipponese Knightship. Afterwards we may meet again at the front somewhere. Then let us fight bravely each other. We have kept the gate keys at the gate room.
> Nipponese Army.

The other note found at the guard house was also dated Rangoon, 29 April 1945:

> To the whole captured prisoners of Rangoon Jail. According to the Nipponese order we hereby give you liberty and admit to leave this place at your own will. Regarding food and other materials kept in this compound we give you permission to consume them as far as your necessity is concerned. We hope that we shall have an opportunity to meet you again at

battlefield of somewhere. We shall continue our war efforts eternally in order to get the emancipation of all Asiatic Races.

Harvo Ito, chief Officer of Rangoon Branch.

A faded Union Jack, the flag of the British Empire, had been honorably used by the prisoners to cover the bodies of their fellow POWs who had died either directly or indirectly at the hands of their Japanese captors. As the men were taken out for burial their bodies were covered with the flag. This hot April morning the same blood-stained flag that had carried so many prisoners to their final rest was raised over the Rangoon Central Jail. It was no longer a prisoner of war camp.

Some of the Indian prisoners went to work painting "Extract Digit" and the "Japs Gone" on the tops of buildings. "Extract Digit" was an old RAF expression. We knew if the airplanes saw the "Extract Digit" sign they would know that Englishmen were down there.

We locked and secured the prison and prepared to await the allies. Chores were assigned for the cook house and a few men were assigned to butcher some of the cattle so we could have meat.

A large tree stood just outside the southeast prison wall. In it we could see a man in Indian clothing. We didn't know if he was friend or foe so we were told to watch him. He eventually climbed down and we thought little more about it. A decade later I was stationed at Denver, Colorado, where I was in charge of the base photo lab. The 10th OSI District was also headquartered there (during the war the OSI was OSS). We handled all the OSI's photo work in our laboratory. I was talking to one of the OSI men one day and he asked where I served during the war. I told him about being in the China-Burma-India Theater and spending 22 months in Rangoon prison camp. He said, "Yes, I know. I was there too."

His story did not square with the facts. I knew all the men in the prison and I didn't remember this man.

I said, "What do you mean you were there? I don't remember you."

He said, "I know you don't. I was sitting up in a tree right above the wall watching you people."

He described the prison and knew about the tree and the wall; things he couldn't have known unless he had been there. I thought it unusual that years later I would meet the same man I saw in that tree outside the prison camp in May 1945.

As we awaited the allies, 50 miles to the north the Japanese Army was battling the British 14th Army near Pegu. On April 30 the Japanese commander at Pegu, Major General Matsui, received an order from Lieutenant General Kimura ordering Matsui's brigade to return to Rangoon "with all speed and defend it to death." Kimura, however, had abandoned Rangoon and was now relatively safe in Moulmein. Matsui resisted the temptation to become an immortal hero in a

Rangoon Prison after the Japanese left.

last-stand battle for the Burmese capitol. Instead he took his band of soldiers into the hills to lick their wounds and fight for Rangoon another day.

Why did the Japanese abandon Rangoon, thwarting the principals laid down by the emperor's army to attack and defend to the death? It certainly wasn't due to an unwillingness to fight. More than half of the 303,000 Japanese soldiers who fought in Burma were killed during the war. The answer is complex but basically political.

The Tokyo high command was bitterly divided about Burma and Rangoon. Kimura and his senior staff officers were afraid of the rapidly-advancing British Army. It is not shameful behavior that they failed to follow the "attack and defend to the death" principal. The main cause, however, of the Japanese army's abandonment of Rangoon points to Commander Kimura's fear of being captured.

As told by Flight Officer Hudson in his book, "The Rats of Rangoon..." On May 1, 1945 all was quiet in the city. Inside the prison camp Captain Myer, an American pilot, was taken to the Air Force compound after all the other prisoners left on the march to Pegu. Myer confided to Hudson that two or three of his fellow Americans were threatening to deal with one Lieutenant Al Bearden, because "they did not want the world to know that the United States Air Force had a stool pigeon in its ranks." They wanted to "do something about it," meaning possibly to kill him. They told Myer of their intentions.

Hudson responded that Bearden was his responsibility but he would lock him up for his own safety if Myer wished.

Bearden was a Texan and a P-38 pilot. The Japanese would bring him in occasionally and put him into a solitary cell next to some new prisoners. Then they'd take him and he would live with the Japanese for a short time. He seemed to be eat better and receiver better treatment than the other prisoners. The indication was that he was a turncoat. After he joined the general POW population I talked with him. He seemed like a nice person but we shunned him. All the Americans had heard the rumors about him giving information to the Japanese. No one, myself included, wanted anything to do with him.

This later bothered me, and it troubled RAF Wing Commander Hudson, too. While Hudson was writing his book, *The Rats of Rangoon* he often wondered if Bearden had really cooperated with the Japanese. This so troubled the British officer that he awoke one night, years after the war, and called Bearden. Hudson has allowed me to recite part of that conversation between the two former Rangoon POWs. Hudson wrote:

> One nagging worry remains. It is Lieutenant Bearden's story that has haunted me for 42 years. What was the whole truth about this Texas pilot who has been branded a Japanese collaborator by so many of his fellow prisoners?

Hudson had heard that Bearden was dead and had been interned in the Sam Houston National Cemetery in Houston, Texas. An A. L. Bearden was listed in the Houston, Texas telephone directory. Calling from Australia, Hudson dialed the number. A woman answered the phone. He asked if there was anyone there would might be related to Lieutenant A. L. Bearden. "He's right here," the woman answered.

The two men visited for a few minutes about the circumstances surrounding Rangoon and the fact the Bearden had failed to keep in touch with other men from the prison. Then the former P-38 pilot suddenly ended the conversation. Hudson was angry and ashamed at himself for not asking what he wanted to know. Standing in his home in Australia he immediately re-dialed the Texan's number. Bearden answered the phone and Hudson asked if he'd mind talking some more:

"Shoot," Bearden said.

"Well, you know most of us thought you were collaborating with the Japs."

"Yes. And I knew you were talking about me. But there's nothing I could do about it. You didn't know what I was going through," Bearden said.

"Were you in trouble when you got back to Calcutta?" Hudson asked.

"No. There was a lot of investigation stuff. First of all there was an Air Force investigation. They cleared me. Then the FBI. . ."

"The FBI?" Hudson said.

"Yes. I checked myself with the people who count. They couldn't have been too much worried about me. I was recommended for the Silver Star after my release. General George Stradimeyer gave me a commendation. And I brought a Japanese rifle back with me. And they gave me a letter to carry home. I've still got that letter."

"Al, it looked to us like you were collaborating."

"I never did. Hell no. I was feeding them false information and they were buying it."

Bearden told Hudson that he had been misleading the Japanese for months and was careful not to get any accurate information from any of the other prisoners because he was having trouble keeping his story straight and didn't want to slip and give the Japanese some useful information. He was aware of how things appeared to the prison population.

"All the time that I was lying to the Japs I had to be real careful. If they had found out they would have slit my throat. So I couldn't tell you people," Bearden said.

"But feelings were running pretty high," Hudson said. "A lot of us were convinced you were a stool pigeon," Hudson said.

"That didn't bother me," Bearden answered. "I had no opinion. I was in a tough spot. When they told you to do something, you did it or else. You know that Hudson, if you wanted to survive."

Hudson certainly did know. He asked Bearden if he could tell the other Ex-Rangoon POWs his story.

"I wouldn't bother. Who would be interested? But do what you like."

At last Hudson had heard Bearden's side of the story. "One point (Bearden) had said, 'I don't want to talk about it. It's all over and done with,'" Hudson wrote. "But the feeling came through as we talked that he had been waiting for a long time to put the record straight."

Roy Wentz, who was also in Rangoon, recalled Bearden in his diary written shortly after the war. Wentz told Hudson that after the war he had written that the entire compound was widely suspicious over the situation. Many believed Bearden as helping the Japanese. However, after talking with Carl Deardslee - another Rangoon POW who was Al Bearden's closest friend and probably the only one in his confidence, Wentz learned that Bearden was finding it tough fooling the Japanese. He was fearful of his inability to stall them much longer. Carl was convinced, Wentz said, that Bearden was really performing a great service to the United States.

On May 2 the allied aircraft were heavily bombing the area south of Rangoon. We thought the bombardment was to help prepare for an assault. About 9:00 a.m. a RAF Mosquito bomber came over the prison, and just as he flew out of sight we heard a loud BOOM. He had blown a hole in the outer compound wall. He didn't know we intended to remain in the compound until we were liberated.

Later that day two RAF officers arrived at the Rangoon Central Jail's main gate. They said they had flown over on a reconnaissance flight, seen the Union Jack, and decided to and check to see if the enemy really had left. The pilot was a wing commander named Saunders and was with the 110th squadron of the RAF. His navigator, a man named Stephens, was with him. Saunders took a boat down to the river to deliver the news to the naval forces that the Japanese had left the prison.

Chapter 19

Liberation

Everyone slept pretty well the night of May 2. We had access to the food stores for several days and had been eating well. On the afternoon of May 3rd a B-24 flying at about 600 feet came straight for the prison with his bomb bay doors open. This made us a little nervous until we realized the bomb bay was loaded with K-rations. They dropped 22 containers of food and medical supplies.

About 4:00 p.m. that day a British war corespondent and a photographer arrived at the prison. They were with the invasion fleet in the gulf. Their boat was making slow headway against the river current so they made their way ashore and walked into the city. They were very surprised to learn that they were the first members of the allied force to arrive at the prison.

They took a good many photographs and talked to several of the men. Then, about 6:00 p.m., we heard the sounds of marching boots. Some of the men had literally been waiting for years for this moment. We opened the doors and in marched a group of soldiers. They strode through the middle of the compound, began firing their guns in the air, and quickly became the center of a long-awaited celebration.

While we had been awaiting allies' arrival the English and the Americans had kidded one another about who would arrive first. The Americans, of course, said it would be the Americans and the English said it would be the British. When the soldiers marched into the compound one of the Rangoon men shouted, "Where you from?" One fellow spoke up and said, "Scotland." Another said "Ireland." Another shouted "Australia." An American hollered real loud, "Scotland? Ireland? Australia? Where's the English?" Everybody got a big laugh out of that.

On the morning of May 4th at 7:00 a.m., 659 ex-prisoners of war marched through the prison gates and down the streets to the dock. We boarded a hospital ship that would take us back to Calcutta, India. The British and Americans sailed first. They were followed that afternoon by the Indians and the Chinese.

It was an overnight trip to Calcutta. Once on board the clothes we had worn in prison were burned. We showered and were given pajamas. The food was excellent but we didn't sleep well the first night. After months of sleeping on wooden benches or the ground, we found the hospital ship beds too soft.

When we docked in Calcutta, the Red Cross met us with ambulances. Some of the men were taken from the ship on stretchers. I don't know why. These same men had been walking around in the prison doing some light work. Granted, they appeared to be in terrible shape. But so did everyone else. The Red Cross gave each man a small bag with a razor, soap, shaving cream, toothbrush and a few other toiletry items. Simple things that before Rangoon each one us would have taken for granted. In the hospital we were placed in a large bay with cots lining the walls. The prisoners who had been marched out of Rangoon on April 25th had already arrived at the hospital. It was good to be together again with these men.

The first thing we did was write home to tell our families and friends that we had been liberated. Some of the ex-POWs had been declared dead and the others missing in action. I know of no one who had been officially listed as a prisoner of war.

The hospital commander told the mess hall to let us have all the food that we wanted. One man ate 18 eggs at a single breakfast sitting.

Everyone made rapid weight gains. I gained 45 pounds in 45 days, was hospitalized for about six weeks, and treated for four different kinds of worms.

Few of the men realized it at the time, but we would require fairly long periods of readjustment to life outside the prison camp. We were short tempered an irritable. Some of the men were evaluated by a psychiatrist. The nurses and hospital staff were wonderful and had a great deal of patience with us.

One adjustment that was surprisingly difficult involved clothing. We were issued new clothes, including shoes. Most of the men refused to wear them in the hospital bay because, after going so long without wearing shoes, they hurt our feet.

Officers were in a separate area from the enlisted men. Lieutenant Cotton would come by our bay and check on us every once and a while. He came by one day and told me he had visited with Captain Sudan. He was in the Indian hospital in Calcutta and was not well. A couple of days later I managed to get a pass and went to see him.

Captain Sudan told me that he had heard from his wife, son and daughter. They were in northern India and were fine. I thanked him for all that he had done for me in the prison camp and told him that without his help I certainly would have died. He said he was glad to be of help. We exchanged addresses. We both faced a long journey home so I told the captain that I might lose his address, or he might lose mine, and I did not want us to lose touch. I asked that if he didn't hear from me in a while to please drop me a note and let me know his whereabouts. He said he would.

I did lose Captain Sudan's address before I got home. I never heard from him again. This is something I have always regretted. Captain Sudan was a slightly-built man but he seemed to hold up very well in the prison camp. The last time I saw him in the Indian hospital in Calcutta in May 1945 he appeared in very ill health. I'm afraid he did not have live very long after that. I would still very much like to contact Captain Sudan's family.

After the war I wrote to the British government in an attempt to locate Captain Sudan but did not receive an answer.

Chapter 20

Home

I left the hospital in Calcutta about June 20, 1945 and flew to Karachi, India, where my service in the China-Burma-India Theater had begun. From Karachi I reached New York City via Casablanca, North Africa, the Azores and Newfoundland. When I reached New York, I called my mother and my family in Mayfield, Kentucky. When I spoke with my mother her voice sounded weak. I asked her if she had been ill. She said that she had, but was fine now. She had received a phone call from the war department on Mother's Day with the news that I had been liberated. She said that was the greatest Mother's Day gift anyone could receive.

I didn't know it at the time but my mother was critically ill with cancer.

From New York I went to Camp Atterbury, Indiana. There orders were cut for a 60-day pass, after which I would report to Miami Beach, Florida for 30 days rest then discharge or re-enlistment. I had been overseas 37 months and had more than enough points for discharge.

I traveled from Camp Atterbury to Louisville, Kentucky, then rode a train the 250-mile trip to Mayfield. On the train I sat next to a lieutenant from Paducah, Kentucky, which is about 30 miles north of Mayfield. He asked me where I was from, and when I told him, he said Mayfield had a war hero and that the town had hosted a big parade for him. The lieutenant said the man had been the leading ace in the middle east and had shot down 18 enemy aircraft. It was Hershel Green, a boy - or a man now - with whom I had gone to high school. This was old news by then, but it was great news to me. I had not been in Kentucky since February 1942 and I had much catching up to do.

I arrived home about 5:00 a.m. on July 6, 1945. My father and two sisters met me at the railroad station. On the way home they told me mother had been ill for some time and had been hospitalized but had returned home. When I got there I could tell that she was very sick.

My mother was one of the most unselfish people I have ever known, always putting her family's needs and wants before her own. I spoke with two local physicians, Dr. Walters and Dr. Usher, about the nature of mother's illness. They recommended she see a specialist. Four days after I returned home we transported mother to Baptist Memorial Hospital in Memphis, Tennessee. My sister Juanita arrived a couple of days later. Mother seemed to be feeling better so I decided to go back to

Ruby Wilson (later, Mrs. Boyd), John Boyd, and Elwanda Anderson, Easter Sunday 1946, Mayfield, KY.

Mayfield that afternoon, July 20. Later that night I went out with friends and had my first date with Ruby Wilson, the girl I later married.

I arrived home after midnight where I met my father. He was leaving to catch a bus to Memphis to stay with mother. I told him I would be in the city the following day, Monday, to bring him home. However, shortly after I went to bed my sister Martha arrived to deliver the news that mother had died from cancer of the esophagus.

I reported to Miami Beach, Florida on September 9th and was discharged from the United States Air Force on October 9, 1945.

Epilogue

John Boyd and Ruby Wilson were married in Mayfield, Kentucky on August 26, 1947. They left Mayfield that same day and spent their wedding night in St. Louis, Missouri before traveling on to Kansas City, Missouri. Kansas City was Lieutenant Walter Cotton's home town. Cotton had secured reservations for the Boyds in a downtown hotel. However, it was playing host to a large convention, several guests did not leave as scheduled and the reservations were not held. Boyd contacted Cotton and told him about the situation. Cotton and his wife Beverly, who had a small baby girl at that time, gave the newlyweds their home for the evening and stayed with Beverly Cotton's parents, who also lived in Kansas City.

This was the last time Boyd saw Lieutenant Cotton. The former Rangoon POW suffered a fatal heart attack a few years after the Boyds visit in 1947. Boyd also lost contact with Cotton's wife and daughter, which he has always regretted.

"Lieutenant Cotton and Captain Sudan did so very much for me while I was in the Rangoon jail and I have always hoped to locate their children and let them know what great men their fathers were and what they meant to me," he said.

The newlyweds traveled to Denver, Colorado where Boyd had obtained a job with his uncle, A. B. Cunningham, who owned White House Cleaners.

Boyd worked as a civilian for about a year then, in 1948, he had the opportunity to re-enter the Air Force as a staff sergeant and to attend the photography school at Lowry Air Force Base in Denver. He took advantage of this opportunity (military training in photography

Lt. Walter Cotton in Calcutta, May 1945.

school that had been his original choice in 1941). The Boyds remained at Lowry AFB for five years where Boyd first served as a photography instructor and later as the photographic supervisor at the base photo lab.

While in Denver the Boyds celebrated the birth of their first daughter, Debra, at Fitzsimmons Army Hospital on July 21, 1952. The next year Boyd was transferred to Germany and two years later their second daughter, Sharon, was born on March 11, 1955.

The Boyds returned to the United States in 1956 when he was assigned to West Palm Beach Air Force Base in West Palm Beach, Florida. Neither Boyd nor his wife liked Florida. Both were interested in relocating closer to their hometown of Mayfield, Kentucky.

By this time Boyd has been promoted to Master Sergeant. The couple decided for John to take his discharge then try to re-enlist at another base closer to their home and families in Kentucky. (Discharged soldiers had 30 days to come back into the military at their current rank. At this time Boyd also had 16 years service in the military and was thinking about a 20-year retirement.)

Boyd knew this was a gamble because if discharged, he would have only 30 days to come back into the service as a master sergeant. But he could do this only if he could find an opening in his Air Force career field, which was photographic supervisor. These positions were scarce since. There was usually only one photo supervisor at each Air Force base. If he failed to find an opening within that 30 day period he could still re-enlist, but not at his current rank.

But as he had so often during his life, Boyd found luck on his side. A few weeks before he left Florida Boyd was in the lunch mess hall with Joe Parsons. A couple of tables away sat a master sergeant who had part of one arm amputated. Although the man had his back to Boyd, he recognized the man. It was Master Sergeant Robert Montgomery, whose arm Colonel MacKenzie had amputated in the Rangoon Prison Camp.

Boyd and Parsons moved to the table behind Montgomery. "If there's anything that gripes me it's all the attention these POWs get," Boyd said in a voice loud enough to be easily overheard. "It just makes me sick. All they did was get caught."

The big master sergeant turned slowly and for a moment didn't recognize his old Rangoon companion. But when Boyd called the man "Monty" he knew at once this was Sergeant John Boyd from the Rangoon Central Jail.

Montgomery was the first American soldier with a disability who returned to the Air Force after Congress passed a law permitting some disabled veterans to re-enlist. President Dwight Eisenhower had personally sworn Montgomery back in the Air Force.

Boyd told Montgomery about his plans to get a discharge then try to re-enlist closer to his hometown. Montgomery said he had recently been stationed at Scott Air Force Base,

M/Sgt. John Boyd at his retirement ceremony. Scott AFB, IL, May 30, 1964.

Illinois, which was only about 200 miles from Mayfield. This was also where Boyd was first stationed and trained as a radio operator after enlisting in the Air Force June 9, 1941. Montgomery told him he had a friend at Scott AFB - a Master Sergeant Heiser - who was in the wing personnel department there. Montgomery suggested that Boyd see Heiser about a photographic supervisor opening.

Boyd was discharged and after failing to find an opening at air bases near both Nashville, Tennessee and Louisville, Kentucky he visited Scott Air Force Base and saw Sergeant Heiser. Boyd introduced himself and explained his need to find an opening in his career field. He also told him he was a friend of Master Sergeant Robert Montgomery.

That changed the conversation.

Sergeant Heiser said that anyone who was a friend of Montgomery was a friend of his. He called the section chief of personnel to see if help could be solicited for Boyd.

Master Sergeant Wynn was the photographic supervisor assigned to Scott AFB. He had 25 years of service and had been talking about retirement. Heiser called this man and asked him if he was, in fact, thinking about retiring. Wynn was a man who didn't mince words. When Heiser called the photo lab the conversation was short:

"Wynn are you thinking about retiring?"

The master sergeant gruffly answered, "Yes."

Heiser immediately said, "OK. Thank you, Wynn," and hung up. Boyd was then assigned to the Scott Air Force Base photo lab as Master Sergeant Wynn's replacement as photographic supervisor, although Wynn didn't actually retire for another two years.

Boyd remained at Scott Field until he retired from the Air Force on May 30, 1964.

Boyd had developed an interest in the real state business. Following his military retirement he returned to Mayfield and worked with Ralph Waltrop of Waltrop and Waltrop Real Estate for three years.

Wishing to be in business for himself, Boyd formed a partnership with regional real estate broker James Majors in 1967. They opened Boyd-Majors Real Estate and located their offices in the former Chester Burn Home at 7th and Walnut Streets in Mayfield, Kentucky.

James Majors and John Boyd began their real estate venture at a time when the real estate business was experiencing what was to be a prolonged boom. They enjoyed a highly successful operation for about 11 years.

Boyd-Majors Real Estate also started several local sub-division construction projects which included the Old Hickory subdivision and the Paddack Hill area north of Mayfield.

Boyd was also active in several civic organizations including the Purchase Area Development District, the United Fund and the American Red Cross. In 1971 Boyd was asked by Charles Murphy, who was chairman of the president selection board for the Graves County Chamber of Commerce, if he would accept the office of president of the Chamber of Commerce. Murphy assured Boyd that the selection board believed that he was the right person for the job. He accepted, offering only a promise to do his best.

During Boyd's term as president of the Mayfield Chamber of Commerce he was instrumental in helping the chamber purchase a suitable lot and construct a chamber building.

Boyd also took an interest in local politics, particularly as they related to the growth of the community. In 1973 the incumbent mayor had decided not to seek re-election. As the April filing deadline approached six people had filed seeking the mayor's position. Boyd decided to enter the race and did so on the final filing day.

In a hotly-contested mayoral primary which drew regional attention, Boyd was elected. This was largely due to the efforts of his wife, family and many very good friends who worked hard during the election. Two men who contributed seemingly endless hours to Boyd's mayoral campaign were A. C. Pickens and George Covington, Sr. Long after his political career came to a close Boyd said, "I'll never forget the help I received from Mr. Pickens and Mr. Covington. They did a great deal to help me in my run for mayor."

The hard work paid off. Boyd was sworn into office on the first Monday meeting of the Mayfield City Council in January 1974.

It proved to be an unusually challenging political year. On August 4, 1974 a Mayfield police patrolman admitted spraying mace into the face of a prisoner. Police regulations prohibited the spraying of mace directly into a person's face. Following a hearing the city council found the patrolman guilty of misconduct, inefficiency and violation of police code regulations. The council felt that some action had to be taken and he was suspended for 10 days without pay.

A few patrolmen had been voicing dissatisfaction from within the police department. These men used the 10-day suspension to further the internal strife. After the city council had made their decision in the mace spraying case some members of the police department held a private meeting. A decision was made to demand that then Mayfield Police Chief Cletus Sullivan be fired and a $100 per month pay increase be granted across the board to the entire police force.

The next morning these demands were presented to Mayor Boyd. The mayor informed the officers that the city would be unable to meet their requests at that time. When they said they would walk out if their demands were not met Boyd asked, "Are you saying you're going to strike or are you saying that you are going to quit your jobs?"

Patrolman Clinton Turner, the unofficial spokesman for the group, told Boyd they knew a strike would result in an injunction that would force them back to work. They intended to quit.

If they truly intended to quit Boyd asked if they would sign a statement to that effect. The men all said they would, so the mayor wrote out a statement in long hand that said in part: "We the following named policemen of the Mayfield Police Department do this day tender our resignations from the City of Mayfield, Kentucky." Boyd then had each man sign the resignation statement. He told them that he didn't want anyone to quit and anyone who contacted him before midnight that day could keep their job. Two of the men did call before the deadline and remained on the police force.

The police walkout took place on August 30, 1974. Sixteen policemen resigned. Thirteen stayed on the job.

The policemen who had turned in their written resignation to the mayor attempted to regain their jobs were rebuffed by both the city council and federal court. The city council voted 7-5 not to employ as a group the 16 ex-policemen who resigned. However, the decision did permit the men to submit individual applications for employment.

The former police officers took their case to the federal court in Paducah, Kentucky. The judge dismissed the case against the City of Mayfield and ruled in effect against the former policemen. The judge ruled that the city had no further responsibility to the policemen after they resigned from their positions.

The men appealed the decision to the appellate court in Cincinnati, Ohio, which also ruled against them.

* * *

During Boyd's four years as mayor the City of Mayfield recorded many physical, budgetary and administrative improvements. In the fall of 1977 the city received a grant for the Community Development Program (CDP). This helped open the door for several other state and federal programs for Mayfield and Graves County. These included the Local Development Cooperation Program (LDC) which has had a tremendous influence in bringing industry to and promoting progress for both the city and county.

The first office of Boyd-Majors Real Estate.

The majority of Kentucky cities applied for the CDP program. Only 16 were chosen, of which Mayfield was number 16.

Dick Armstrong, who at the time was with the Purchase Area Development District, handled the mountain of administrative paper

Mayor John Boyd, City of Mayfield, KY 1975.

work required for the application grant. Mayor Boyd, with help from the Kentucky Municipal League and other sources, lobbied for the grant proposals acceptance.

The Community Development Program could have been administrated one of three ways: (1) by the city council; (2) through the Purchase Area Development District; or (3) the mayor and city council could appoint an independent board to administer the program. They chose the third option. Mayor Boyd appointed the independent board which was approved by the city council.

Dick Armstrong and Stan Lampkie emerged as the top two candidates for the position of CDP executive director. Both were considered by the mayor to be highly qualified and both had the proven administrative skills to successfully handle the job. Boyd sought the advice of Henry Hodges, executive director of the Purchase Area Development District, about filling the CDP's top post.

After much consideration Mayor Boyd recommended Dick Armstrong for executive director of the Community Development Program. The City of Mayfield and Graves County have been well serviced by Armstrong's tenure as executive director.

Others occurrences during Boyd's term as mayor included: the city property annexation of 1,650 acres, a federal facility study made to study water and sewer systems and establish methods for upgrades and improvements, the purchase of a 100 acre site for city landfill, a collective $89,000 pay increase for city employees, the influx and extermination of more than 2,000,000 blackbirds, a city ordnance update study by Murray State University, a transportation study and request to widen Highway 45 to four lanes and construct a by-pass, construction of a new press box and locker room facilities at Mayfield High School and various other accomplishments.

The Kentucky Department of Transportation told the mayor and city council that before the traffic projects could be considered they would need to close north 8th and north 7th Street along with a few other streets to two-way traffic. This was needed in order to accommodate the flow of traffic in and out of the downtown area. This is one reason for the present one-way streets in Mayfield.

* * *

In 1977 the city's budget was running short and to meet its financial obligations the mayor and city council decided that the city would have to raise taxes. Boyd was determined not to be re-elected first then raise taxes. The city council and the mayor's office agreed that a payroll tax was the best and fairest way to generate the additional needed income for the city.

Boyd was also serving on a committee for the National League of Cities. He attended meeting in Washington D. C. and had the opportunity to visit with Kentucky Senator Wendell Ford. Boyd mentioned to the senator that the council and mayor's office would pass a payroll tax about 30 days before the election. Senator Ford's comment was, "Say that again." He was again told about the plan to pass a payroll tax before the election. The senator said: "John, that's political suicide." The mayor acknowledged that it very well could be, but he would not be elected first and then raise taxes because the city needed the money now. Ford's answer was not encouraging: "Good luck."

The council did pass the ordinance to raise the payroll tax three-quarters of one percent. It also increased the mayor's annual salary from $3,600 to $7,500 and increased the council member's salaries from $30 per month to $100 per month (these monies were made available when the city judge and the city prosecutor's offices were eliminated by the state legislature).

Ford was correct. The tax increase proved to be political suicide. Boyd along with several council members were defeated in the May primary election.

During the campaign Boyd had tried to take his argument for higher taxes to the people: "I had tried to explain to the public why we needed the tax increase," he said. "Then after my defeat (by almost a two-to-one margin) I asked myself several questions, one of which was about the tax. I wondered: Did the people really understand that we needed the tax ? Or did they think we just wanted more money to spend? In a democracy the majority rules. Apparently the majority of the people of Mayfield did not want an increase in the payroll tax."

The new mayor had been elected on the promise of no more taxes.

He was going to be given the chance to make good on his campaign pledge. After the May primary election Boyd requested that the council members resend the payroll tax. The mayor argued that this was the only way to demonstrate to the public that the tax really was necessary.

The council did resend the tax increase but it was short-lived relief. The new council and new mayor were forced to re-instate a payroll tax the following year.

Political rhetoric such as the kind that helped defeat him still bothers Boyd: "What politicians will say to get elected has always troubled me," he said. "You always hear things like 'No more taxes!' and 'Listen to the people!' when the people saying it often have no idea whatsoever what is actually needed or why it is needed.

"The politician does what he does for the benefit of votes," Boyd added. "The statesman does what he does for the good of the country or the county or the city. There is a tremendous difference. I never felt like I was a politician."

In November 1977 as Boyd's term as mayor was coming to a close he received the *Mayfield Messenger's* annual Citizen of the Year Award. It was the first time the award had been given to any elected official and Boyd considered the award a tremendous honor.

Concerning the Citizen of the Year selection for 1977 the *Mayfield Messenger* said:

> The citizenship award is presented annually to the person judged to have contributed the most to the community during the past year. A prerequisite for the award requires volunteer efforts "above and beyond the call of duty."
>
> This year marks the first time the award has been presented to any elected official. Presentation of the award was deliberately delayed until after the May 24th primary election in order to eliminate the display of any inferred political preference prior to the election. The award is intended to recognize outstanding efforts toward making the community a better place in which to live, not an endorsement of political views.
>
> While many residents may disagree with Mayor Boyd's policies, no one can deny his total dedication to the obligations of his office. Finishing his fourth year in office, Mayor Boyd had been one of the most energetic and productive mayors in the city's history, in our opinion.
>
> Under his leadership, the city has received a total of $1,956,684 in federal and state grants for civic projects.

These monies have been used to install new sidewalks in the downtown area, begin construction of a new city-county swimming pool through the cooperation of the Graves County fiscal court, install six new public tennis courts, establish a city-county Park Board and park program, resurface 10.4 miles of streets, increase ambulance service outside the county, begin a new Senior Citizens Center, adopt a detailed budget with monthly reporting service, 32 new elderly housing units, new stop signs, turn lanes and traffic survey, selection of Mayfield for final application for (a) $498,000 community development grant, and others.

During his term as mayor Boyd said his work was aided by a good city council and excellent supervisors in all departments - supervisors who were well qualified and very much concerned and dedicated to what was best for the city and the employees in their departments. Their cooperation was a strong asset to Boyd's work in the mayor's office.

The four years Boyd served as mayor (during which time the mayor's annual salary was $3,600) were also some of the best years in

When threatened with the firing squad on August 3, 1943, I asked myself two questions: "If I had been able to live, who would I have married?" and "Would I have had a family?" The answer to these questions is in the photograph: Front row L-R: Sharon Shrene (daughter) with Boyd Shrene, Laura Carter, Catherine Shrene, Michelle Carter, Debra Carter (daughter) with Jenny Shrene. Back row L-R: Ruby Boyd (wife), sons-in-law John Shrene and Michael Carter.

the real estate business. Not long after Boyd's mayoral term ended the real estate business crashed. In 1979 interest rates rose to 21 percent and the real estate business plummeted. During this difficult time he again asked himself the question he asked the night of August 3, 1943: Was it all worth it? The answer, he said, then and now, was and is, "Yes, it was worth it. There are many good people in the world." Boyd found his friends, family and business associates a source of great strength during the real estate collapse.

"During this period the encouragement, strength and help that I received from banks in Mayfield along with friends such as Bill and David Driver, George Cook, James R. Cash, Fredrick Blume and the best and most loyal partner a man could have, James Majors, was immeasurable. Again I'd say, Yes, it was worth it."

Today, John Boyd remains active in the real estate business and in civic affairs. He holds what he considers the most important duty of his life as that of an elder in the Seventh and College Church of Christ in Mayfield, Kentucky, where he also teaches Sunday School.

From a burning B-25 over Meiktila, Burma to a successful business and political career in Kentucky, Boyd says the Lord has showered him with blessings.

"Through it all the Lord has blessed me with a good wife, a wonderful family and many good friends. My blessings have been too many to count."

Sources and Acknowledgments

For the study of dates and detail to recall the events of my tour in the C-B-I Theater of war during World War II, the author is grateful to the following publications and individuals who allowed the use of their information. It was invaluable in writing this book.

Lionel Hudson, *The Rats of Rangoon*, Leo Cooper. England 1987.

Ian Morrison, *Grandfather Longlegs*, Fabor & Fabor Ltd. London 1947.

Robert Hammond, *The Flame of Freedom*, Leo Cooper. London, England 1988.

K. P. MacKenzie, *Operation Rangoon Jail*, London, England 1954.

John (Tim) Finerty, *All Hell on the Irrawaddy*, Anchor Publications, (Cablegood Ltd.) Bagnor Regis, Great Britain 1985.

Hugh Crumpler, *Ex-CBI Roundup*, San Diego, California July 1989.

Joseph W. Cunningham, Rockville, Maryland.

K. F. (Jack) Horner, Tampa, Florida.

Perry Marshall, Troy, Tennessee.

Roy Pagani, London, England.

Donald Humphrey, St. Louis, MO.

EX-POW Rangoon, Burma, Historical Directory.

The Strait Times, Singapore, Republic of Singapore.

Appendix I:

Burma's Major Ethnic Groups

The following is a list of major ethnic groups in Burma. The figures are estimates based on information from the U.S. State Department and leaders of some of the ethnic groups. Burma's government has no census and no population figures, but the total population is believed to be about 37 million.

Ten Groups belong to the National Democratic Front:

1. Arakan: About 1.5 million in western Burma. Cut off from other insurgent ethnic groups by the Burma Army, which controls central Burma. Six political factions within the state, the largest of which is the Arakan Liberation Party. No military force.

2. Kachin: About 1 million in northern and northeastern Burma. Strong political and military organizations. Close ties to U.S. through World War II, when Kachins fought with U.S. troops in Burma, and influence of pre-war Baptist missionaries.

3. Karen: About 2.5 million in south-eastern Burma. Strong ties to England that stem from British colonial days. Baptists, Buddhists and 7th Day Adventists.

4. Karenni: About 300,000, also known as Red Karens. Sometimes referred to as Kaya. Strong political organization but dependent on Karens for military support. Baptists and Roman Catholics.

5. Lahu: Population size is not available. Hill tribe is Shan State. Buddhists, Animists and Baptists.

6. Mon: About 500,000 located in south-eastern Burma along border with Thailand. Strong military force but internal political disputes have kept the Mons from being effective in ethnic politics.

7. Pa-O: About 800,000 scattered throughout Shan State. Close ties with Shans and Karens. Primarily Buddhist.

8. Palaung: About 700,000 primarily in Shan State. Predominantly Buddhist.

9. Shan: About 3.2 million primarily in Shan State in south-eastern Burma. Several political and military factions vie for power among the Shans. Pre-dominantly Buddhist but some Baptist and Methodist influence.

10. Wa: About 250,000 in extreme eastern Burma, with influence reaching into Yunnan Province of the People's Republic of China. Wa State under military and political control of Communist Party of Burma and Tai Revolutionary Council.

The other three major groups are:

11. Burman: About 25 million concentrated mainly in south and central Burma. Control government, military and most businesses. Primarily Buddhist.

12. Chin: About 5000,000 located in western and northwestern Burma. No organized political or military groups. Animist and Buddhist.

13. Naga: Population size not available. Extreme northwestern Burma. Practiced headhunting until shortly after World War II. No effective political or military organizations.

Appendix II: Rangoon Ex-POWs

A Flight Of No Return

by Sunny Young

A streak of silver in the sky
The engines roar, propellers try
To lift the giant screaming plane
Above the mountains drenched with rain
Black ominous clouds and gale winds blow
Amid the ice and swirling snow
As plane and crew, with every breath
Tries to win a fight with death
To climb above the snow capped peak
A place not for the very weak
The plane is in a mighty grip
The crew can hear the metal rip
As suction lifts them like a kite
Above the peaks into the night
Then, just as quickly dropped like snow

22nd Bomb Squadron 1st Reunion: May 1987. St. Louis, MO.

Into the jutting rocks below
Time has rune out for plotted goals
A cry aloud, "God save our souls
A crash like Thunder, a flash of light
Then silence in the blackened night
Crumpled engines, wings, and tail
Help pave the "Hump's" Aluminum Trail
A dog tag here, a jacket there
A picture worn by love and care
A parachute unopened lay
No time to jump, No time to pray
In this far, forgotten place,
of jungles, mountains, rocks and space
The wreckage lay like broken toys
Discarded by mischievous boys
And boys they were of tender years
And families weep in silent tears
To know the sacrifice they made
The part their gift for freedom played
Lieutenants, captains, sergeants too
Privates, maintenance, or crew
Whatever rank, Whatever job
They did their best with each heart throb
Some gave their lives to save a friend
A brother to the very end
They gave their lives, so we might live
What more can any person give.

John Boyd and Roy Anthony Stevens (RAS) Pagani together at the reunion, 50 years after liberation.

Silent Sleep

by Lloyd Klar

Her great roaring engines are long silent,
Her guns are pitted with rust.
Olive drab paint is flaking and faded,
Turrets are covered with dust.

She sits and waits for her crewmen,
Those young men from another day.
Fifty long years have passed and gone
Since they all went away.

Where have all those young men gone,
Those boys she knew so well? They took her there and brought her
back,
What stories they can tell.

Some are buried in foreign lands,
War records tell the place.
"Killed in Action" the official words,
Or just "KIA" to save space.

Others went down in a fiery crash, Just where, no one can tell;
Over Burma jungles or China cliffs,
No markers where they fell.

Others came home, the war was over,
We dissipated like the dew,
Then separately we all went our ways
Back to the lives we knew.

To All Young Heroes

by Sunny Young

So many lives have tone unrewarded
So many dreams gone unfulfilled
So many days and nights of sorrow
So many young men maimed and killed
So many lie in foreign countries
In unmarked graves, never to be found
Because the treacherous Himalayas
Consumed them and their planes when they went down
Life must go on, time heals the broken hearted
The "Hump" still stands, in solemn mystery pressed
The jagged peaks splitting the Horizon
With snow, they hide the secret in their breast
And storms still rage with screaming winds of terror
The rain still gushes to the valley floor
But with the rage and fury of the mountains
It can not hurt these young men any more.

T/SGT ROBERT BICKNELL JR. (TEX) was born June 27, 1922, and lives with his wife Doris in Alexandria, LA. He served as a flight mechanic on CG-4A (glider) with the Troop Carrier, 1st Air Commando. On Sunday night, March 1944, they left their base in India for Burma. They had two CC-4A gliders behind a C-47. Somewhere behind the Japanese lines, their two rope released itself from the C-47 (reason unknown), and they crashed in the jungle. His pilot, Lt. Charles Liston, was seriously injured and died en route to Rangoon. Ted Yackie and "Pappy" Hart were with him when he died.

Bicknell visited Liston's family in Adel, IA, after he was discharged in November 1945 in North Carolina. He met his mother, sister and a sister-in-law. He had a wonderful family.

Bicknell was with three English soldiers and they were captured the night of March 10, 1944. The three Englishmen were shot and one died in Rangoon from his wounds.

When several men were marched out of Rangoon, Bicknell was one of them. He was liberated April 29, 1945, after serving about 14 months (or 419 days). Freedom at last!

T/SGT JOHN W. BOYD was born Dec. 12, 1918, and lives with his wife Ruby in Mayfield, KY. He was assigned to the 341st (M)BG, 22nd Sqdn. and served as a radio operator in a B-25.

His crew consisted of the following: pilot, Lt. Charles W. McCook; copilot, Lt. Nathaniel L. Hightower Jr.; navigator, Lt. Henry J. Carlin; engineer, Sgt. John E. Leisure; radio operator, Tech. Sgt. John W. Boyd; and gunner, Sgt. Sidney Burke.

In an experimental skip bombing mission on Aug. 3, 1943, their B-25 bomber was the last of three to go in on the target at tree top level. With heavy ground fire an explosive shell started a fire in the bomb bay and Lt. McCook then pulled up to about 1,000 feet. The heat was so great that Sgt. Leisure (with chute on) released the emergency hatch and motioned he was going out. All chutes were seat type.

Boyd motioned Sgt. Burke out of the turret and helped him with his chute. By this time the plane was below 800 feet and in a landing approach angle. The tree tops were very close as he put his arms through the straps, with hand on the rip cord and standing over the hatch, he closed his legs and went through the bottom hatch standing straight up without the chute being strapped on. He pulled the cord as his head cleared the door. The chute opened, his head flew back and his feet hit the ground at the same time. The plane hit in the same field and blew up, killing the four remaining crew members. Boyd was paralyzed from the fall, immediately captured and beaten. He was a prisoner in Rangoon Prison Camp, Rangoon, Burma for 23 months and liberated by the British army on May 3, 1945.

Sgt. Leisure and Boyd were the only two to get out of the aircraft. Sgt. Leisure died in Rangoon Prison Camp during the cholera epidemic in June 1944.

1/LT M.B. BURKE lives in Tampa, FL. He was a navigator on an aircraft leading flight "D" in formation and bombing the railway station at Rangoon. A few seconds later they were hit by what he thought to be flak. The #2 engine was out, but not feathered; #3 and #4 were on fire and feathered. There was fire in the fuel cell behind #3 and in the bomb bay; #3 fell off wing and there was large hole where fuel cell used to be. The radio operator (master sergeant) was hit in his left arm, shattering his wrist and nearly severing his hand from his arm. The electrical system and interphone were out, and the bail-out order was given.

Lt. Walsh, Lt. Derrington, M/Sgt. Montgomery, Lt. Burke, Lt. Levine, Lt. Coffin, Capt. Meyer bailed out in that order. They landed approximately 20 miles northeast of Rangoon. They contacted Levine and made plans for escape. (Bail-out occurred at approximately 1135 I.S.T.). They decided to find Monty to help him and were surrounded by Burmese and taken to the village. They found Monty and did what they could, which wasn't much, and gave him sulfur-drugs and morphine. Due to being armed, they were not badly treated by the Burmese. They were picked up by the Japanese at about 1700.

S/SGT SAMUEL A. CROSTIC (BUD) was born March 24, 1922. He served as a gunner with the 10th AF, 7th BG, 9th BS. He was shot down over Pymaunna Junction (March 1943) and was captured approximately four days later by natives (who turned him over to the Japanese).

He traveled by truck and train to Rangoon. The train was bombed en route by B-25s. Arrived at Rangoon to find the rest of his crew, Higgenbottow, Jensen and Baggett, already there. Jensen and Baggett were sent to Singapore, while Higgenbottow and Crostic remained in Rangoon until the Japanese attempted to move them in May 1945. Consequently, they were then released.

He lives with his wife Ruby in New Smyrna Beach, FL.

S/SGT S.L. DOW was a staff sergeant in a B-29. He flew over Rangoon at 21,000 feet; the target was the railroad station. Bombs away, then was hit. He still doesn't know if they were hit or if it was their own bombs that were put in the bomb bay wrong, but the ship was full of holes. The #3 engine was on fire; #2 engine was smoking very badly, and the airplane was losing 2,000 feet per minute.

Dow jumped out when the airplane started to go haywire, then went up forward to the rear bomb bay. He was going to jump out there, but gas was coming out of the front part as they were closing them. He was afraid of fire in the inside of the plane, so went to the rear exit. He jumped out at 15,000 and landed on a small island 25 miles southeast of Rangoon.

He was picked up by Burmese and then turned over to the Japanese. All this happened on Dec. 14, 1944. He was taken to a village and slept over night there. He ate cake, drank tea and was brought to Rangoon in the morning. Dow was at the MP headquarters for one an a half days.

He was brought to Rangoon Prison on the night of December 16. Everybody was safe. One man was wounded (radio operator for plane B-29), his hand had been shot off at the wrist.

Dow lives in Gardiner, ME.

S/SGT DAREN ENGEL was born Dec. 31, 1923. He served as a tail gunner in a B-25 and was assigned to the 10th AF, 12th BG and 83rd BS.

He was shot down near Mykteta, Burma on Oct. 8, 1944, and arrived at Rangoon Prison five or six days after, along with John Russell, the only other survivor of his crew and Richard Moore a P-38 pilot. He spent the next 90 days in solitary confinement spending his birthday, Thanksgiving, Christmas and New Years in that cell block. He was then transferred to Block 8 for the remainder of his confinement.

He especially remembers Johnny Hurt or Block 8 "Mess Sergeant," Wing Commander Hill, their appointed CO for Block 8, Cliff Emery, who took the major responsibility for caring for the sick and injured in Block 8 and, of course, Dick Moore and John Russell.

After they were liberated by the English ground forces, he returned to the military hospital in Calcutta via an English Hospital Ship and eventually was returned to the States and discharged from the Army Air Force.

Engel has been retired since October of 1978. He and his wife Billie divide their time between Springfield, Oregon and Yuma, Arizona.

1/LT G.M. ETHERINGTON (BUD) was born Sept. 14, 1921. He lives with his wife Margo in Birmingham, AL. Etherington served as an engineer in a B-29 with the 20th AF, 20th Bomber Cmd., 40th BG, 45th BS. Crew members: pilot, Bob Shanks; copilot, Harold Fletcher; bombardier, Bob Benedict; navigator, Julian Cochran; flight engineer, G.M. (Bud) Etherington; CFC gunner, Nick Ogelsby; radio operator, Ferrell Majors; left gunner, Arnold Basche (deceased); right gunner, Walter Lentz; tail gunner, Henry Pisterzi and radar operator, Lewis Sommers (deceased).

On Dec. 14, 1944, 11 planes from the 40th BG made two passes over the target in Bangkok, but they were unable to get a visual sighting because of cloud cover. They then proceeded to Rangoon to bomb the rail yards.

Under protest they were carrying a mixed load of 1,000# and 500# bombs. Immediately after bombs away, there was a tremendous explosion (bombs from their formation) which they later learned damaged every plane in the formation and four planes were lost.

They had two engines on fire (which they managed to extinguish) and much other damage. Another engine was hit and they finally feathered it. Somehow, they managed to fly about 20 minutes, but when the last engine started to burn, they all bailed out somewhere over the delta land of the Irrawaddy River.

Etherington came down near a small village and tried to negotiate for a boat. Within a few hours he was captured by a Burmese WO who turned him over to the Japanese. After three or four days their whole crew was back together. They were 11 days getting back to Rangoon, traveling by boat, foot, truck and rail. On Christmas Day they arrived at Cell Block #5 and on Jan. 12, 1945, they were moved to Compound #8.

Their treatment was typical of what all endured: interrogations, threats, beatings and near starvation. In late April he was with the group who were marched north and east. Finally, after their guards had left them, they made contact with the British 14th Army. A few days later they were in the 142nd Gen. Hosp. in Calcutta.

T/SGT GRADY M. FARLEY was born Feb. 23, 1919. Farley served as a flight engineer in a B-24 with the 10th AF, 7th BG, 493rd BS.

They were shot down Nov. 14, 1943, over north Burma. Farley and E.S. Quick were the only ones that got out of the plane. Quick was captured that day and Grady roamed around 14 days before the natives captured him and turned him over to the Japanese.

He was carried to Rangoon and held in the Rangoon MP HQ for 13 months. They were moved to the central prison in Rangoon and placed in cells for three months, then moved into a compound (he thinks it was Block 8) that was mostly AF personnel.

He returned to college after the service at Auburn University, Auburn, AL, and married after graduation in 1948. Retired in January 1981 from the Tennessee Valley Authority and lives with his wife Pat in Russellville, AL.

CPL BILL FLYNN served as a radio operator in a C-46 with the ATC, India-China Wing. On Nov. 7, 1943, they departed Sookerating, Assam Valley for Kinming, China. On the return flight they encountered bad weather and radio problems, so flew far south of the normal route to find better flight conditions. By dawn they were running extremely low on fuel and opted to bailout rather than ditch airplane.

The crew split up and Flynn hooked up with Charlie Montagna and headed west. They were "befriended" by the Burmese and betrayed to a Japanese search party. Taken through Mandaly to Maymyo for approximately two months. They were joined by Col. Gilbert, Jean Lutz, Chris Morgan and "Bo" Bowman. Transferred to Rangoon in early January 1944.

Flynn lives in Falls Church, VA.

COL DOUGLAS G. GILBERT was born July 8, 1909. He lives with his wife Micheaux in Warrenton, VA. Gilbert served in the Infantry. In late November 1943 he was assigned as a liaison officer to the 112th Inf. Regt. of the Chinese Division, then operating against the Japanese in the Hongquong Valley, about 60 miles south of the American liaison headquarters under Gen. Boatner at Ledo, Assam, India.

On November 22 he returned to the forward command post after two or three days at the supply headquarters seven miles to the rear, contacting Gen. Boatner's headquarters. The moment he arrived at the command post, heavy firing continued throughout the night during which a soldier inside the dugout got excited by the firing and fired his rifle killing their guard at the entrance. He could not communicate with the Chinese and in the jungle anything that moves draws fire so he stayed put. At dawn the many troops moving about the command post proved to be Japanese, and they were soon discovered and made prisoners.

He was kept in the command post area for several days as the Chinese attempted to retake the area, during which time he had a physically rough interrogation and served as a trussed up parapet for a soldier's fox hole. Fortunately, they were in a depression so the bullets flew overhead. After a few days he was evacuated by train south of Maymo where he joined Jean Lutz, Chris Morgan, Bo Bowman, Bill Flynn and Charlie Montagna. Morgan was critically ill but after urging, the Japanese let them take him with them on a stretcher on their evacuation to Rangoon by truck.

In April 1945 the Japanese marched all of them who were fit enough, north for four nights before abandoning them as the British 14th Army drew close. That same day they were strafed by the allied fighters but lost only Brigadier Hobson. That night, Jean Lutz made contact with the British and they were evacuated, half that night and the remainder the next day.

DUDLEY W. HOGON JR. was born May 4, 1923. He was a pilot in a P-51 with the 10th AF, 311th BG, 307th BS and was imprisoned from Nov. 27, 1943 to May 4, 1945. Retired, he lives in Augusta, GA.

LT DONALD M. HUMPHREY was born July 23, 1920. He was a pilot in a F-4 and served with the 10th AF, 9th Photo Cmd.

They were hit over Rangoon by ack-ack; with one engine out, they were pursued and shot down by fighters. Captured May 5, 1943, he spent 30 days in city jail, Rangoon Burma; 40 days in solitary at #5

Compound, Rangoon Prison; and the balance at Compound #6. He was recaptured above Pegu by Slim's 14th British army in March out of Burma. Humphrey was liberated May 1, 1945.

He lives with his wife Virginia in St. Louis, MO.

2/LT GUS JOHNSON was born June 25, 1922. He was a bombardier in a B-24 and served with the 10th AF, 7th BG, 436th BS. He was captured Oct. 26, 1943 and liberated in May 1945.

They were hit by the Japanese "Tojo" fighters over Rangoon, lost at least one engine, then a running gunfight for 50 minutes at which time the Japanese fighters started using two fighters each pass, instead of one. Using two was a new tactic for them and they misjudged a pass from 7 o'clock low, with one fighter flying through the waist windows. Their B-24 broke in half, the front portion ending up in a glide inverted, with no tail section. The navigator (Waller) exited through the astrodome and Johnson followed, very close to the jungle near G.W.A. Bay.

After finding his way out of the jungle, he was picked up by native Burmese and turned over to the Japanese army. Held captive in New Law Courts (solitary) and became #1 KP. Roy Wentz and Joe Wells arrived about Thanksgiving or Christmas and they have been friends ever since. They all returned from Rangoon on the HMS *Karapara* (hospital ship) to the 142nd Gen. Hosp.

He lives with his wife Sylvia in Stuart, FL.

CAPT CLARENCE A. KING (CLANCY) (RET) was born May 17, 1918. He served as a navigator in Consolidated B-24 D with the 10th AF, 7th BG, 493rd BS. King was captured Oct. 14, 1943 and liberated on April 29, 1945.

He was captured near Maubin, Burma after bailing out of a burning plane. Other survivors were: Harold Goad, Bill Schrader, Gene Sawyer and Russ Gebert.

King was liberated by the British near Pegu after a forced march from Rangoon. Japanese guards fled during a night of heavy strafing by British and American fighter planes. British Brigadier, who had been the ranking officer in the POW camp at Rangoon, was killed during the strafing.

Flown by C-47 to Calcutta and spent approximately three weeks in the 142nd Gen. Hosp. there. He was flown by C-54 to La Guardia Airport with brief stops at Karachi, Abadan, Cairo and Casablanca en route.

Arrived home in Great Falls, MT in early June to find that he had been declared MIA when shot down and officially dead one year later by the War Department. Memorial services were held in the spring of 1945 at the church where he attended Sunday School as a boy.

He was discharged from the service in January 1947 after several operations at Letterman Gen. Hosp. in San Francisco. He completed his education at the University of Oregon in 1949. For him George Burns said it best: "If I had know I was going to live this long, I'd have taken better care of myself."

He lives with his wife June in Eugene, OR.

S/SGT WALTER LENTZ was born Sept. 19, 1917. He was a right gunner in a B-29 with the 20th AF, 40th BG, 45th BS. Lentz was captured Dec. 15, 1944 and liberated on June 6, 1945.

He was on Robert Shanks crew and they were on the disastrous mission on the railroad yards of Rangoon, Burma on Dec. 15, 1944. They bailed out about 100 miles west of target and were picked up instantly by the natives who turned them over to the Japanese. It took them 10 days to get back to the prison (December 25th, what a Christmas!).

As liberation neared the Japanese blew up ammo dumps around the prison. One morning they were gone taking all prisoners that were able to walk, and leaving a note on the prison gate as follows: "We have guarded you according to Japanese knighthood and hope to meet you on another battlefield."

There was a Charles W. Whitely in their compound. He remembers him well because he was from Charlotte, NC. He has tried a couple of times to locate him, but with no success.

He lives with his wife Vena in Hudson, NC.

1/LT JOE LEVINE was born April 7, 1922, and lives in Southfield, MI. He was a bombardier/navigator in a B-29 with the 20th AF, 40th BG, 25th BS. He was captured on Dec. 14, 1944, and was liberated in May 1945.

Their target was Rangoon Railroad Marshaling Yards. During bombing run, just after "bombs away," the aircraft was hit. Three engines were out, one on fire. The wing and bomb bay were on fire also. All 12 of them were able to bail. The engine nacelle and right wing fell away before the plane hit the ground. Burke, Montgomery and Levine got to a small Burmese village. Montgomery's hand was hanging by a thread, and Levine gave him morphine and sulfa powder in the wound and applied a tourniquet to his upper arm. Monty seemed to be in shock.

About two hours after the Burmese promised to help them escape (at night), a Japanese lieutenant with a squad of about eight men approached the village. He surrendered for the three of us.

The Japanese took them by boat to a small police (?) station where the rest of the crew were being held. All of them were made to stand with their hands tied behind their backs. About six hours after bailing out it was dark. Levine had been attending Monty's tourniquet for the first three to four hours, but then he lay in a heap with no attention. Both Walsh (engineer) and Levine kept complaining about Monty, and both of them got a few whacks on the head for their trouble. Finally, about seven to nine hours after the bailout, a Japanese doctor severed Monty's hand, tied the blood vessels and bandaged the stump. About that time, they were told to lie down on some beds.

At dawn they were awakened and marched outside, their hands still tied. He thought for sure they were going to be beheaded or shot (he was hoping for the latter). Instead they were loaded on a truck and brought to the POW camp. They joined crew members of the other four planes in a large yard. There were newsreel cameras recording the capture of B-29 crews. It seemed as if they hadn't had any food or drink since they were taken prisoners. Monty was not with them, but they found him later in the cell with them.

Levine was with the group that marched out of Rangoon and was liberated by the British five days later.

S/SGT B.A. LUKAS (BEN) was born May 21, 1915, and lives with his wife Betty in Niceville, FL. He was a gunner in a B-24 with the CBI Cmd., 10th AF, 7th BG, 493rd BS.

On Oct. 18, 1943, the target was the Tongoo Rail Road Yards. South of Monday they were attacked by Japanese fighters. Ascending, hit bomb bay and plane caught fire. The crew evacuated with plane on fire and shortly thereafter exploded.

Severely wounded with head wounds, he was picked up by Burmese natives who wrapped him up in his parachute and took him to a civilian police station in the proximity of Monday. Because his name, rank and serial number were entered on a police blotter when the Japanese came into the village, they had no alternative but to take him to Japanese Intelligence Headquarters in Maymo and subsequently to the Rangoon Jail. He was liberated April 30, 1945.

SGT JOSEPH C. McCLUNG was born July 31, 1920 and lives with his wife Dean in Redding, CA. He was an engineer gunner in a B-24.

He was shot down and captured Nov. 27, 1943, while bombing Rangoon, Burma. They were bombing the railroad shops where the engines were worked on. They were flying from India, which was a 14 hour round trip flight, and there were 53 bombers on this mission. His plane lost two engines, therefore, they couldn't keep up with the other planes. The Japanese fighters got them, and he jumped at 12,000 feet.

McClung was first put into Rangoon Federal Law Courts in the basement. He was in a 9 x 12 room where he stayed for eight months. One of his crew died there. Then they were moved to Section 8 where he spent five months after which he went to the compound.

He was on the forced march up the Burma Road with the other boys, but never knew many of them. McClung was liberated April 29, 1945.

On Dec. 23, 1979, he went on a kidney machine. He has been on CAPP, the tube in his side, since March 1980. If his health continues, he plans to attend the reunion in St. Louis.

M/SGT FERRELL T. MAJORS was born May 13, 1918, and lives with his wife Marion in Fullerton, CA. He served as a radio operator/ mechanic in a B-29 with the 20th AF, SAC Cmd., 40th BG, 45th BS.

On Dec. 14, 1944, they were hit by an explosion of their own bombs upon release over secondary target, Rangoon, Burma (Bob Shanks crew). Flying on one engine they were able to go about 100 miles from target before bailing out. All crew members were okay, except Copilot Fletcher who sprained both ankles upon landing. They were turned over to the Japanese the same day by Burmese People. They were friendly, but feared Japanese reprisals. The Japanese took everything except coveralls and shoes. He received a beating for not having a revolver in his holster. He had no clips so did not carry a gun.

They were turned over to Japanese guards who took them back to Rangoon 11 days later, after many interrogations and several beatings. In late April after spending four and a half months in captivity, he was taken from prison and marched to Pegu four days later. The guards then left them on the run to escape the British army. That night he was picked up by the British and flown back to a hospital in Calcutta where he gained 40 pounds in one month. He was then flown home, given a 60 day furlough and reassigned to Supply in Santa Monica.

He was released from the service in October 1945. His health has been very good; there are no problems from malaria or dysentery.

CHARLES MONTAGNA was born April 8, 1919, and lives with his wife Ann in Mission Viejo, CA. He was a copilot crew chief in a C-46 (Curtiss Cmd.), CBI, Air Trans., 29th Trans. Gp., 99th Trans. Sq.

They were flying aviation gasoline from India to China over "the Hump" for Gen. Chennomb's 14th AF. They left Kunming, China at one o'clock in the morning on Nov. 7, 1943, for their return flight to India. Through a series of unfortunate and unexplainable circumstances, their flight lasted through the night. As the first signs of daylight appeared in the east, their fuel was exhausted. Their pilot, F/O Parris gave them the option of either bailing out or attempting a crash landing. It was decided that a crash landing would be impossible to survive in view of the jungle terrain.

Consequently, the entire crew bailed out and in the jungle below he was reunited with his radio operator, Billy Flynn. For a short time, they attempted to locate and join up with the rest of their crew, but to no avail. Flynn and Montagna spent two days in the jungle trying to find somebody or someplace to help them out of their dilemma. What they ran into was a group of native Burmese who marched them through the jungle into a Japanese camp. He was liberated April 31, 1945.

CAPT RICHARD D. MOORE was born May 7, 1923, and lives with his wife Elsie in Waco, TX. He was a pilot in a P-38, with the 10th AF attached to British 3rd TAF, 459th BS.

Mission on Sept. 8, 1944, was by 16 P-38s with one belly tank and one 1,000 lb. RDX bomb. The target was the jettys in the river at Monywa, Burma.

They arrived on target approximately 8:30 a.m. Flak was very heavy 40mm about 3,500 feet and 90mm at their altitude of 9,000 feet. The plan was to peel off in a steep dive and release bomb at 3,000. He began his pull out on schedule, but then sustained a direct hit on the leading edge of the right wing between the engine and pilot's nacelle. The aircraft was difficult to control due to violent turbulence caused by a large hole. He regained control at about 200 feet. The fuel tank in right wing was ruptured and the engine quit. An attempt to maintain altitude on single engine failed, and they crash landed with only scratches to show.

Moore found he was on the edge of a small village and hid under a bush until 11:00 a.m. He was discovered by a small boy who could see under the bush (it was a long time before he liked children again). He shouted and the bush was immediately surrounded by Burmese and Japanese. He was beaten, kicked and tied up with a stick thrust through his elbows in back and his hands tied in front, then tossed in the back of an ox cart and taken to Monywa.

The next month was spent being interrogated in Monywa, Shwebo, Meiktilla and Mandalay. He learned to speak some Japanese and some Burmese by talking to the guards. He found out, after many beatings for refusing to speak or lying, that they had all the scoop on the squadron anyway, including an almost complete roster of personnel.

Finally reached Rangoon and his story became a carbon copy of all the others. He was liberated May 6, 1945. Reached home, he thought. After two weeks he became partially paralyzed due to malnutrition and spent the next four months in and out of hospitals. Other than bad teeth, high blood pressure and loss of hair, he wasn't hurt a bit.

2/LT CHRISTOPHER W. MORGAN was born Sept. 3, 1923, and lives with his wife Constance in Old Bridge, NJ. He was a fighter pilot in a P-51, served in the USAAF and was assigned to the 10th AF, 311th Ftr. Gp., 529th Sqdn.

On Oct. 16, 1943, he was forced down, crash landed in a Burmese rice field and evaded capture for five days. On the fifth day he joined with "friendly" natives who promised to lead him back to India. Instead, they led him into an ambush of Japanese soldiers.

After literally running the gamut for almost 1,000 miles, he arrived at Rangoon Prison and spent three months in solitary confinement. He was then released to a compound area comprised mostly of British and some American personnel. For the balance of his imprisonment, he witnessed almost daily his fellow prisoners dying from malnutrition and lack of medical care.

On April 25, 1945, they were marched from Rangoon to Pegu, where they were intercepted and liberated on May 1, 1945, by the British 14th Army.

M/SGT RICHARD A. MONTGOMERY was born Sept. 19, 1917, and lives with his wife Margaret in Riverside, CA. He was a radio operator in a B-29 and served with the 20th AF, 58th Cmd., 40th BG, 25th BS. He was captured Dec. 14, 1944, and liberated in May 1945.

1/LT CHESTER E. PAUL was born May 30, 1921, and lives with his wife Shirley in North Hills, NY. He was a pilot in a B-29 and served in the CBI Theater in the 20th AF, 40th BG, 45th Sqdn. On Dec. 14, 1944, target-Bankok Bridge; bomb load-mixed load of 1,000 pounds plus 500 pound bombs with instantaneous fuses.

The target was cloudy, and since this was primarily a training mission, photo's were required. They went to secondary target, the Marshaling Yards at Rangoon. Apparently some bombs crossed to ajectories and deteriorated under the squadron.

Their plane, #831, was in a flat spin with both inboards on fire. Neither manual efforts by Lt. Treimer and Paul, nor automatic pilot could regain control. An alarm was sounded but failed to activate. Bail out was ordered over intercom and was heard. The nose wheel was lowered (bomb bays were still open) and all bailed out of the cabin except Lt. Treimer whom Paul last saw at the wheel well ready to jump. Treimer did, however, have blood on the side of his head, and Paul never saw him again.

They were fired upon while descending and Lt. M. Larsen and Paul later compared bullet holes in their chutes while in POW camp. Larsen won with many more than Paul had. Paul landed in a circle of Burmese natives and Japanese soldiers. He was taken at once to the city lock-up for questioning and several days later transferred to the POW compound. His best recollection of the city lock-up was a sign giving rules to be observed and ending with the admonition: "Those will be cleanliness everywhere."

They marched (pulling ox carts) 60 miles north to Pegu. The Japanese abandoned them when they ran into the British 14th Army. A Burmese runner made his way through Japanese lines (falling back toward them) to the British who sent a contingent to bring them out. While waiting for them, they spent a night in a Burmese village which was infiltrated by Japanese, some of whom were asleep right besides them.

Liberated May 3, 1945, he was flow back to Calcutta and several weeks later, home.

CPL CURTIS F. PRITCHARD was born Sept. 3, 1906, and lives with his wife Wilma J. in Asceola, ME. He was a crew chief in C-46 - Cargo 47 & 87, Gen. Hoag Command, 1st Trans. Gp., 6th Trans. Sq.

On Jan. 30, 1944, while on a mission flying over the Hump from Kunming, China to Chabria, India, they ran into a storm, got lost and ran out of gas. They had to bailout into North Burma. He landed in the Irrawaddy River and was captured by the Burmese army and turned over to the Japanese.

He was taken to Mandalay then to Maymyo, Burma for about two or three weeks, then back to Mandalay for one day. He was picked up at midnight, with five Chinese and five Japanese, and taken to Rangoon until April 30, 1945. Then the Japanese took several men, including Pritchard. While on a march they were captured by the British army and taken to 'Calcutta India Hospital for two weeks until he gained 30 pounds, then on to America.

CAPT J.L. RUSSELL lives in Dedham, MA. Their B-25 was attacked by four zeros and set on fire. Russell was hit by a bullet in the left leg and bailed out. The plane crashed while still on fire, four were killed and two escaped, Russell (radio operator) and the tail gunner. They were shot down and captured by Burmese on Oct. 6, 1944, and entered Rangoon Prison on Oct. 14, 1944.

S/SGT FRANCIS E. SAWYER (GENE) was born Dec. 3, 1918, and lives with his wife Mildred in La Crosse, WI. He was an engineer/gunner in a B-24D and served in the 10th Army Air Corps, 7th BG(H), 493rd BS(H).

The day was Oct. 14, 1943; the target was the Pazandaung Boat Works at Rangoon, Burma. They were to fly with the 9th Sqdn. that day. Little did he realize that would be the last mission he would ever fly. They dropped their bombs at Rangoon around noon; antiaircraft was heavy.

After they left the city, Jap fighter planes jumped them. The plane, on which he was gunner, was hit in the bomb bay fuel tank. The midsection of the plane was set ablaze. All men by him made ready to leave. Sawyer bailed out and seconds later, the plane exploded and broke in half. Five of the 10 aboard the plane survived.

They were approximately 45 miles west of Rangoon. After landing, he was picked up by Burmese villagers, who turned him over to the police. They took him by boat to Pantanau, and there he met the four officers of his crew. They were questioned and slapped around. The next stop on their boat trip back to Rangoon was Maubin. After two nights there, they arrived in Rangoon.

On the eve of Thanksgiving Day 1943, while he was in solitary, the RAF accidentally bombed the prison, followed by the 7th BG. Both raids killed a few men and damaged buildings. In December of 1943, they were finally put into a compound with other prisoners. Disease was all over the prison. They were given shots for typhoid, tetanus, bubonic plague and small pox (more for the Jap's self-preservation and to keep their slates clean, should we be liberated).

On Oct. 30, 1944, he was officially dead by War Dept. records and next of kin were notified. They were given orders by the Japs on April 25, 1945, to go on a march. Early in the morning on the 29th, those who could walk were stopped in a woods about 61 miles north of

Rangoon. They were near Pegu, Burma. The Japanese leader gave them a note telling them they were free by order of the Imperial Emperor; then, he and his men took off in full retreat. They were about five to seven miles from the British front lines. Confusion reigned at this point, but later that evening, an American officer stole into the British perimeter and made their true identity known. They were picked up by the British 14th army, spent two comforting nights with them, and then were flown to Calcutta. The Americans went to the 142nd Gen. Hosp.

He arose from the "dead" on April 30 or May 1, 1945. After spending a week in Karachi, they started for New York City, and landed at LaGuardia Airport that evening on May 28, 1945. They were home! For them the fighting was over. He had only 35 missions, but was satisfied.

1/LT WILLIAM C. SCHRADER was born Aug. 5, 1918, and lives with his wife Ann in El Paso, TX. He was copilot in a B-24 and served with the 10th AF, USAAF CBI, 7th BG, 493rd BS. He was captured Oct. 14, 1943.

They went on a bombing raid to Rangoon. The target was a boundary on an island just south of Rangoon. Fighters were around them during the bomb drop. Shortly after that, the fighters made a couple of head on passes at them, but a twin engine 1-45 came in under their right wing and hit them in the bomb bay tank setting it on fire. They tried to get out of formation and finally got it in a shallow right diving turn. The controls had almost been completely burned out.

Sawyer got out the right waist window, but was pretty badly burned as flames were pouring out of it. After they got home, the navigator in the plane behind them said that was the last he saw of them as the fighters were all over them.

Schrader doesn't know how long the tail and the right wing and nacelle stayed together. This threw Goad and Schrader out through the cockpit canopy, safety bed and all. King and Gefert got out through the nose wheel door and the last he saw of the top turret gunner he was trying to get out of the turret, but he doesn't think he made it before it came apart. Schrader passed out when he was thrown out. When he came to he could see parts of the plane all around him, but some distance away. Delayed opening parachute, but not long enough. A twin engine fighter strafed him a couple of times before he got on the ground.

He sprained both ankles when he hit and was picked up by Burmese about 15 minutes later. That evening the Japanese arrived and things got rough. The next day they took him to the tail section the

Burmese had already buried. There was a big bulge in the end of the tail near the turret, I guess they were all in a bunch when it hit. They were taken to Rangoon City Jail for two days, then transferred to Central Jail. A British invasion force liberated them on May 9, 1945. They were put on a hospital ship and taken to Calcutta.

2/LT FRED K. SCHWALL was born Sept. 12, 1921, and lives with his wife Jean in Key West, FL, from November to June and in California from June to November. He was copilot in a B-24 and served with the 14th AF, CBI, 308th BG, 324th BS. He was captured Nov. 26, 1943, and liberated April 30, 1945.

They went down about 100 to 250 miles northeast of Mandaly. Crossed the front lines about April 29, 1945, while being moved towards Thailand from Rangoon.

CAPT ROBERT C. SHANKS was born Dec. 25, 1919, in Grand Prairie, TX, and lives with his wife Letha in Grand Prairie, TX. He was a pilot in a B-29 and served with the 20th AF, 58th BW, 40th BG, 45th BS. His recount of circumstances is about the same as Etherington and Cochran. He was captured Dec. 14, 1944 and liberated May 4, 1945.

SGT WILLIAM H. THOMAS was born Oct. 27, 1923, and lives with his wife Maxine in Cummings, KS. He was a tail gunner in a B-24 and served with the 14th CBI, 308th BG, 324th BS. He was captured in November 1943 and liberated in May 1945.

Crew members were pilot, 2nd Lt. N.G. Kellam (deceased); copilot, 2nd Lt. Fred K. Schwall; navigator, 2nd Lt. John D. Marcello; bombardier, 2nd Lt. George E. Harman; flight engineer, S/Sgt. Perry Marshall; radioman, S/Sgt. Thomas E. Seneff (deceased); assistant engineer/gunner, Sgt. Charles W. Perry (deceased); armorer gunner, Sgt. Noman E. Albinson (died in prison camp); armorer gunner, Sgt. William H. Thomas; and armorer gunner, Sgt. Don Z. Davis.

Their B-24 was forced down in northern Burma (Akyab) on Nov. 27, 1943. The pilot's chute opened in the plane so they decided to go down together rather than parachute out when the fuel was exhausted as originally planned.

No one was injured in the landing, but the bombardier was shot in the back during gunfire exchange when the Japanese captured them the next morning.

They marched and carried the bombardier for about a week. When they reached Mandalay, the Japanese furnished a truck for transportation to the Rangoon Prison. After about 45 days in solitary, they were transferred to Cell Block 5. Their treatment was same as all the airmen: beatings, starvation diet, etc.

About April 24, 1945, he was with the POWs who were marched north toward Pegu. After three nights of marching, the Japanese guards left them in a wooded area. They attracted the attention of an observation plane and shortly after they were bombed and strafed by four allied (British) planes.

The next morning they were picked up by Gurka soldiers of the British 14th army. After spending the night with the British, they were flown to the Army hospital in Calcutta.

S/SGT KARNIG THOMASIAN was born April 8, 1924, and lives with his wife Diana in River Edge, NJ. He was left gunner/electrical specialist in a B-29, XX Bomber, 40th BG, 45th BS.

They took off, 13 proud B-29s from their base in Chakulia, India on a bright, sunny morning, Dec. 14, 1944, after they had been briefed by Col. Blanchard the night before. Karnig had been talking with part of his crew, Vernon Henning, top gunner CFC; Leon McCutcheon, right gunner, engine specialist; Richard Brooks, radio operator; August Harmison, tail gunner; Robert Dalton, radar operator and Karnig as left gunner, electrical specialist.

They were discussing what they were going to do during the weekend after this mission. It was never to become a reality. Their primary target, a bridge leading to railroads in Bankok, Thailand was clouded over, so they proceeded to their secondary target, Rangoon Railway Yards. "Bombs away!" There was a terrific explosion in the air under their formation. Their mixed load of bombs had collided, exploded, causing their own planes to drop from the skies.

The explosion pushed their plane into a complete flop and ended in a flat spin with three engines on fire. Everywhere he looked it was like peering through a red filter. Two bodies went by the open bomb bay door. Karnig jumped and found himself hanging upside down by his leg straps, for he was unable to buckle his chest strap. His left hand was injured. Above him were four chutes and one below him. Six of his crew did not make it, including his pilot, "Doc" Treimer. He landed on the ground on the other side of the Rangoon River in the rice paddies.

Natives surrounded him and the Japanese soldiers were close behind. They tied his hands and led him to the river bank where he saw his copilot, Chet Paul. Dazed, they were taken to the city jail where they were interrogated and beaten. Next day they were moved to the Central Rangoon Prison, where they were to stay until liberation. He was in solitary in Cell Block #5 for three months, and from time to time, he signaled guys in Block #6. In the fourth month, he was moved to Block #8. He knew he had to keep himself vital as possible to survive, so he volunteered for anything and everything. He cooked, gave shaves and haircuts with a handmade blade made from an old barrel hoop. However, he contracted deep, painful ulcers in his left ankle, which made walking difficult. He couldn't wear shoes. Because of this he was left behind when the Japanese forced a march of the mobile prisoners just a few days before liberation.

They were found and liberated by British Gurkhas on May 7, 1945, and taken to a British hospital ship. They were then transferred to Calcutta, hospitalized and sent home on an Army Transport, Priority 2.

J.I. THOMSON lives in Moshi, Tanganyika Territory. Beating up sampans near mouth of Mayo R., he noticed high rad. temperatures and headed for home informing his number 1 over R.T. (radio). The engine rapidly lost power and he had to land. He set fire to aircraft and made for the hills. Was at large for 10 days using emergency rations and food from villages. He was caught by INA while trying to cross lines with help of some Burmese. He was taken to Japanese, then to INA Camp north of Akyab where he was kept for about nine weeks. He was brought to Rangoon just before monsoon.

1/LT FRANK H. TILCOCK was born March 22, 1920, and lives with his wife Mary in Tallahassee, FL. He was a pilot in a P-38 during the CBI Theater with the 9th Recon Sqdn. He was captured Sept. 19, 1943.

He was on a photo mission over Rangoon, Burma and was to photograph the docks, railway station and Mingladon Airport. He had made two passes when he saw two Japanese fighters over his left shoulder. He firewalled the throttles on the P-38 and headed for home.

After about 30 minutes, he couldn't see the fighters and throttled back to cruise. All of a sudden a noise like hail on a tin roof occurred and his instrument panel disappeared and smoke poured into the cockpit. His left engine was on fire. Time to bailout! As he climbed out of his seat, the plane exploded and he passed out. When he came to, he knew he was falling, how long, he didn't know. He pulled the rip cord and passed out again. When he came to, the fighters were circling my chute. They did not shoot. He went through some clouds then landed in a tree, which bent enough to allow his toes to touch the ground. He got out of his chute and retrieved it by cutting down the tree with his machete which was in the seat of his chute.

He walked through the jungle, following a stream for two days. On the third day he was surprised by some Burmese. They acted friendly and appeared to be helping. They walked for several hours, by-passing many villages. At dusk, they led him to a hut on the outskirts of a village, where he was met by Japanese soldiers. They put him in an ox cart and drove onto a paved road. He was then put into a truck. They drove all night and arrived at Rangoon. He was interrogated several days and was in solitary for 86 days. After which, he was put into the compound with the other prisoners.

In April 1945 the well prisoners were marched out of Rangoon Prison at night. Tilcock thinks the forced march lasted for three nights. The fourth days they were resting in some trees and the Japanese guards left them. Some small Army recon planes flew over and attracted their attention. Soon after, they were strafed by British fighters. They all split! That night he hid in a ditch covered with leaves and heard troops and tanks passing by. The next day the British encountered them. He was returned to Calcutta by air and it was all over, thank God.

S/SGT LELAND H.W. WALTRIP was born Nov. 17, 1921, and lives with his wife Lenora in Cottonwood, AZ. He was a tail gunner in a B-25 and served with in the CBI Theater with the 12th BG, 434th Sqdn.

On May 29, 1944, on a flight over Burma, they were skip bombing the Railroad north of Pegu and were hit by ground fire. The ship started burning and he was told to bailout over the mountains by Pilot John McCloskey. The copilot was killed on bailout. Captured within three days, he was taken to Rangoon City Jail for about one month, then put in solitary for about eight months, then in Block 5 until they were marched north, turned loose and liberated on May 3, 1945. There is no need to write about mistreatment as everyone that was there knows all about it. There were six in his crew and only four made it back.

LT ROY A. WENTZ was born Nov. 20, 1920 and lives in Wilmington, DE. His wife is deceased. He was a navigator in a B-29 and served with the 10th AF, 7th BG, 9th Sqdn. He was captured in December 1943.

Led two groups of B-24s to bomb Rangoon on Dec. 1, 1943. They were attacked by fighters, lost two engines and parachuted near Bassein. He was taken by boat to Rangoon and imprisoned at New Law Courts

Building. Moved to Rangoon Central Jail about July 27, 1944, where they were kept isolated in cells until Jan. 27, 1945. They were moved into an open compound. Liberated by the British on May 2, 1945, and taken to Calcutta by boat.

American POWs

Rangoon Burma Jail

Baggett, Owen
Benedict, Cameron R.
Bicknell, Robert (Tex)
Bowman, Mel
Boyd, John W.
Brooks, Richard
Changnon, Harry M.
Cochran, Julian C.
Coffin, Lionel F.
Crostic, Samuel R. (Bud)
Derrington, Robert
Dow, Stanton L.
Edwards, F.R. (Bud)
Englel, Daren
Etherington, Galpin (Bud)
Farley, Grady M.
Fletcher, Harold E.
Flynn, Bill
Funk, Gerald
Garrett, Hubert (Ross)
Gilbert, Douglas
Harmon, George E.
Hogan, Dudley W. (Bill)
Horner, K.F. Jack
Humphrey, Donald M.
Johnson, Gus
King, Clarence (Clancy)
Larsen, Norman
Lentz, Walter R.
Levine, Joseph
Lukas, B.A.
Majors, Ferrell
Maloney, Raymond R. (Murph)
Marshall, Perry
McClosky, John H. (Jack)
McKernan, James M.
Montagna, Charles (Monty)

Montgomery, Richard (Monty)
Moore, Richard D.
Morgan, Christopher
Oglesby, Nicholas P.
Parris, Joe E.
Paul, Chester E. (Chet)
Pisterzi, Henry E. (Hank)
Pritchard, Curtis F.
Pugh, Fred M.
Rooney, William
Sawyer, Francis
Schwall, Fred
Shanks, Robert E.
Thomas, Bill
Thomasian, Karnig
Tilcock, Frank
Trinkner, Edward
Waltrip, Leland
Wells, Joe
Wentz, Roy
Whitely, Charles W.

Widows of POWs

Burke, Bettie (Marion)
Davis, Dorothy (Don)
DuBose, Nina E. (Alan)
Greene, Pat (Harlan)
Higginbotham, Lorraine (Tadix)
Johnson, Jane (James)
McClung, Dean (Joseph)
Radcliff, Mary (Smith)
Schrader, Ann (William)

United Kingdom

Checkley, Bert
Coffin, L.
Davies, Arthur
Davies, Les
Davis, John

Dyson, Arthur
Finnerty, Major J.
Foster, Marshall
Fowler, Norman
Frank, Leon
Gibbs, F.G.
Gibson, Alec M.
Holloman, Fred C.
King, G.
Knights, Norman
Leese, W. (Bill)
Leggate, George
Matthews, William
McIlveen, John
Morgan, Fred
Nicholls, Alf
Pagani, R.A.S.
Guilliam, Tom
Ramsey, Raymond
Ratcliffe, George
Rix, A. John
Rogers, Arthur
Rose, Lewis W.
Sammons, Alan E.
Shortis, John A.
Smith, John
Spurlock, Ken
Stibbe, Phillip
Stier, Len
Stott, Frank
Tippey, Jack
Wilding, W. Alan

International

Besley, Harvey
Coppin, James
Corbett, R.J.
Desmond, Gerald
Eastgate, D.L. (Lofty)
Emeny, Clifford

Ferguson, Charles D.
Guayle, Douglas
Harvey, G.L.J.
Hudson, Lionel (Bill)
Lissenberg, S.R. (Lissy)
Mills, Douglas
Osboldstone, Eric
Reid, John
Trigwell, E.W.M. (Wally)
Wilson, John J. (Hank)
Woods, Malcolm S.

Appendix III: American POWs Honor Roll

Rangoon, Burma

WWII, CBI Theater

Died in Air Crash in Rangoon

Birkmaier, Theodore A.
Blank, William T.
Burke, Sidney
Burness, Irving
Carlin, Henry J.
Conway, Robert W.
Cummings, Chester L.
Dalton, Robert E.
Gerber, Howard L.
Hall, Stacey B.
Harmison, August A.
Henning, Vernon
Hightower Jr., N.L.
Lancaster, Charles
McCarthy, James M.
McCook, Charles W.
McCutcheon, Leon L.

Rice, Allen J.
Teimer, Wayne
Vermillion, James A.

Died on Way to Rangoon Prison

Dohn, Norman P.

Died in Rangoon Prison

Albinson, Norman
Allen, Roy B.
Almand, Paul E.
Angel, Robert
Aubuchon, Urvern A.
Bodell, Edward R.
Briggs, Everett
Cummings, Harold E.
Gonsalves, Elias, E.
Hopes, Thomas E.
Kavanagh, Robert L.
Jordan, Francis
Kelley, John P.
Kellner, Joseph
Lavery, John E.
Leisure, John E.
Malok, Albert L.
Ortmeyer, John
Pittard, Charles
Redmon, Jack L.
Rodriquez, Frank
Soules, Halloran E.
Westberg, Lofty
Wright, William
Yackie, Julius

Died in Years After Liberation

Basche, Arnold H.

Bearden, Aaron L.
Beardslee, Carl M.
Bishop, Louis W.
Bockman, Clifford H.
Bray, Clifton L.
Burke, Marion B.
Cotton, Walter E.
Davis, Don (Kid)
Doyal, Horace B.
Gerbert, Russel C.
Goad, Harold W.
Greene, Harlan B.
DuBose, Allan D.
Hall, Robert C.
Hart, Fletcher E.
Hastings, Alvin L.
Higginbotham, T.E.
Hubbard, John W.
Hunt, John W.
Johnson, James S.
Kellam, Newton
Korotkin, L.
Lutz, Charles J.
Marcello, John D.
McClung, Joseph
McGivern, James B.
Meyer, Cornelius C.
Miller, Donald V.
Niland, Edward F.
Parmalee, Burton
Perry, Charles
Quick, Ernest S.
Radcliff, Smith W.
Redd, Charles H.
Schrader, William C.
Seneff, Thomas
Sommers, Lewis W.
Wagoner, Obra
Walker, Steward B.
Walsh, William
Whitescarver, J.T.

Wilson, George

22nd Bomb Squadron Veterans Killed In Action

The following is a list of names of 22nd Bomb Squadron Veterans Killed in Action that is carved on "The Monument to the Aviation Martyrs in the War of Resistance Against Japan" in Beijing, China:

Abeel Jr., Robert S.
Altman, Walter
Alton, WIlliam J.
Baldanza, Joseph A.
Barron, Robert K.
Bolduc, Gerard J.
Bonnell, Donald G.
Brokaw, James W.
Brown, Albert L.
Brown, Harold E.
Brown, Walter C.
Browne, Albert R.
Burke, Sidney
Caldwell, Robert E.
Caldwell, Robert D.
Carlin, Henry J.
Casper, Harlan G.
Causey, Gordon R.
Clare, Thomas H.
Clements, Sim B.
Cockrill, James M.
Cook, Myron L.
Cousins, Allan M.
Cromwell, Herbert
Crooke, Willard E.
Danfield, George
Davis, Richard
Deverse, Anthony P.

Dickinson, Samuel C.
Doucette, Walter J.
Dunham, Thomas T.
Duploa, Robert C.
Elkins, Rudolph
Evans, Charles C.
Feld, Philip
Ferguson, Charles F.
Finks, Robert E.
Flack, John A.
Floyd, Alva H.
Fowler, Jesse E.
Fox, Melvin P.
Gaither, Herschel
Ganoe, Finley H.
Gardner, James H.
Gowell, Robert W.
Gray, Robert M.
Greenstein, Max
Hamer, James J.
Hansen, William L.
Harding, Hampden W.
Harrison, Vernon M.
Herforth, Henry J.
Hewitt Jr., Joseph P.
Hickey, James W.
Hightower Jr., Nathaniel
Hirsch, John G.
Hodgers, Norman O.
Hodgkinson, George M.
Hopper
Horn, Guy V.
Howard, WIlliam A.
Hyde, Merrill R.
Jacobs, Lawrence G.
Jaggers, Russell
Jones, Charles
Ketchum Jr., Yale A.
Kokonis, James
Larkin Jr., George E.
Lawrence, Irvin H.

Leisure Jr., John E.
Lemich, John
Levee, Jessie C.
Mandello, Anthony M.
Manson III, John N.
Marich, Nicholas
Markham, Donald F.
Michel, Theodore, J.
Mihalichko, Joseph
Miller, Dale M.
Montes, Ralph J.
Morse, Harold B.
Myers, Walter S.
McCook, Charles W.
McDonough Jr., John F.
McGraw
McIninch, Vernon A.
McMahon, Neal R.
Newsome, Sidney S.
Nielson, Fay L.
Nordahl, Lynn C.
Norton, John P.
O'Dea, James L.
Parkhurst, Clarence H.
Pipkin, Ralph E.
Plante, Napoleon E.
Poleselli, Viviano

Propst, Robert L.
Radke, Lee
Rymer, Robert R.
Sandini, Alfred R.
Saterfield, Curtis L.
Schenk, Ernest B.
Schusterbauer, Bertram A.
Seaver, R.N.
Shupe, John W.
Simonic, Paula, J.
Simonnetti, Phil
Smith, Everette W.
Smith, Forman F.
Smith Jr., Thomas J.
Stocker, John J.
Sutton, Frank R.
Ullman, Frank E.
Wanderer, Stephen A.
Watkins, William J.
Weaver, Charles M.
Webster, Floyd E.
Welch Jr., John J.
White, Samuel, M.
Worland, Louis F.
Young, Marshall
Zera, Thomas P.

Dibrugarh • Tinsukia • Futao (Ft. Hertz)

Sibsagar • Ledo

Ledo Road

Chaukan Pass 7980'

Pangsheng

16200

Yenyuan •

Likiang •

Weisi •

Shingbwiyang

Pangsho

Pangsham

NAGA HILLS 9840

Maingkwan

Walawbum

Sumprabum

Mogaung Valley

11429

Klenchwan •

Y U N N A N

Erh Hai

Kohima •

Tanai

Mansi

Yunlung •

Tali •

Yunnanyi •

To Kunming and Chungking

Turu Gap

Myitkyina

Paoshan •

Burma Road

Tsuyung •

Homalin •

Mogaung

Tengchung • 8547'

Shunning •

Maingkaing • Mansi

Lungling •

Kingtung •

Tamu •

Mawlu

Nabu

Katha

Bhamo

Namkham •

Mienning •

Chenyuan •

Pinlebu •

Sittaung

Wuntho •

Inywa

Tigyaing •

Shweli

10608 +

Kingku •

Indaw • Kawlin

Mawlaik •

Thabeikkyin

Tagaung

Mabein

Mong Mit

Mogok

Bawdwin • Lashio

Kunlong

Wa States

Mokiang •

Namtu

Man Hpang

Papien

9680 +

Zigon • Ye-u • Kinu

Hsipaw

Möng Yai

Ningerhi •

Szemao •

Shwebo •

Madaya

Nam Pan Hie

Gokteik

Myinge

Lantsang

Monywa

Sagaing

Maymyo

8500

Cheli •

Amarapura

Mandalay

Kehsi Mansam

Myingyan •

Kyaukse •

Kume

Laihka

Kengtung •

Pakokku •

Sinu

Thazi

Payangazu

Lawksawk

Kenglikam

Möng Yawng

Muongsin •

Aukpadaung

Meiktila

Yamethin

Taunggyi

Kengtung

Salin •

Pyawbwe

Aungban

Myindaik

Mawkmai

Mong Pan

Mong Hsat •

Banhouelsai •

Minbu •

Magwe

Yenangyaung

Hsihseng

Southern Shan States

F R E N C H

An Pass

Pyinmana

Loikaw

Chiengsen •

I N D O C H I N A

Yenanma

Allanmyo

Karenni

Chiengrai •

Thavetmyo •

Toungoo

8610

Mawchi

6530

Prevao •

Nagor •

Nan •

Tamu •

Taungup

Prome

Pyu

Doi Intanon 8470

Chiengmai •

Lampang •

Prae •

Taungup Pass

Minhla

Mesarieng

Hawt •

4846 +

Kyangin •

2690

Papun •

Utaraditra •

Henzada •

Thatrawaddy

Kyaikto

Dawna Range

Sawurgalok •

Danubyu •

Insein

Pegu

Tak (Raheng)

Bisnulok (Pitsanulok)

Lomsak •

Bassein •

Rangoon

Martaban

Moulmein

T H A I L A N D

Bejnaburau (Petchabuni)

Maubin •

Thongwa

Labutta •

Yapon

Rangoon River

Amherst •

To Bangkok and Singapore

TENASSERIM

Kalegauk Island

Gulf of Martaban

0   50   100   150

STATUTE MILES

22nd BOMB SQUADRON 341st BOMB GROUP

Standing, L to R:
> Capt. Thadd Blanton, Pilot, *"Doolittle Raid,"* now deceased;
> Lt. John Lemich, Co-Pilot, shot down 10 Sept. 43, Naba Junction, no survivors;
> Lt. McGraw, Navigator, shot down 10 Sept. 43 Naba Junction, no survivors;
> Lt. Joseph Cunningham, Bombardier, shot down over Hong Kong on Oct. 42, mission, walked out, later returned to the states.

Kneeling, L to R:
> S/Sgt. George Danfield, Engineer, shot down 10 Sept. 43, Naba Junction, no survivors;
> T/Sgt. John Boyd, Radio Operator, shot down 3 Aug. 43, Meitkelia, 21 months Rangoon Prison.

Arrived Larachi, India July 25, 1942.

Mayor Boyd and Senator Ford in Mayfield, Kentucky 1976.

L to R; Governor Carroll, Judge Crider, Jim Brien, Judge Castleman, and Mayor Boyd in Mayfield, Kentucky, 1977 at the presentation of a State Grant to the city of Mayfield.

John and Ruby Boyd, 1991.